CHRISTIAN WORSHIP
AND
TECHNOLOGICAL CHANGE

CHRISTIAN WORSHIP AND TECHNOLOGICAL CHANGE

SUSAN J. WHITE

ABINGDON PRESS
Nashville

CHRISTIAN WORSHIP AND TECHNOLOGICAL CHANGE

Copyright © 1994 by Abingdon Press

This book is printed on recycled, acid-free paper.

Library of Congress Cataloging-in-Publication Data

White, Susan J., 1949–
    Christian worship and technological change/Susan J. White.
      p.   cm.
    Includes bibliographical references and index.
    ISBN 0-687-07663-3 (pbk.: alk. paper)
    1. Liturgics.   2. Technology—Religious aspects—Christianity.
  I. Title.
  BV178.w47   1994
  264—dc20   94-20989
                                                  CIP

Scripture quotations, unless otherwise noted, are from the New Revised Standard Version of the Bible, copyright © 1989 by the Division of Christian Education of the National Council of the Churches of Christ in the USA. Used by permission.

Cover art is a detail from Pieter Bruegel, "Turmbau zu Babel," and is used by permission of the Kunsthistorisches Museum, Vienna, Austria.

Book design by J. S. Laughbaum

94 95 96 97 98 99 00 01 02 03 — 10 9 8 7 6 5 4 3 2 1

MANUFACTURED IN THE UNITED STATES OF AMERICA

For Kenneth
who encourages the faith of so many through
countless acts of "justice, courtesy, and love"

CONTENTS

PREFACE AND ACKNOWLEDGMENTS

This book is about two things in which I am passionately interested: Christian worship and technology.[1] Although I am trained and employed as a liturgist, my interest in technology is perhaps more comprehensible than my interest in the public prayer of the Christian church. I was born at the beginning of a period of heightened technological enthusiasm, and to be "modern and up-to-date" was something embedded within my family's code of honor. Our house was the first in the neighborhood to have a television set, a washing machine, and a dishwasher, and the advent of each of these devices (and the awe and admiration they produced in my schoolfriends) is locked in my memory. But I was almost never taken to church as a child, and I cannot remember a single experience of common worship from my youth. If I believed in a higher power, one with the ability to transform the quality of daily living, it was very probably in the power of technology. When my interest in the church and its worship was finally aroused, I was working at that mecca of technological advancement, the Massachusetts Institute of Technology, and I was immediately faced with the difficulty of how to integrate the two worlds of which I was a part. This book is part of that continuing effort at a correlation of worlds.

As I worked on this book, various people approached me and, when told the subject of the book, said either "But liturgy and technology have nothing to do with each other!" or "Oh good! Now the minister will be able to run the overhead projector!" This book presupposes that liturgy and technology *do* have something to do with each other, but it is not about "how to run the overhead projector." It is about the ways in which technology and technological thinking have influenced planning for, studying, and participating in Christian public worship. It argues that technology can and does alter our perceptions of how the liturgy is constructed, how it changes, how it shapes the faith of the believer, and how it functions within congregational life. And because I agree with Ian Barbour that "the human consequences of technology are the result of a two-way interaction between technical possibilities and social institutions,"[2] this book is also about the ways in which the liturgy as a social institution has influenced the course of technology.

An author accumulates an enormous number of debts, both personal and intellectual, during the course of writing, and this author is no different. At the early stages of this work, I was given great encouragement by several colleagues, especially Wiliam Seth Adams of The Episcopal Seminary of the Southwest and Paul Bradshaw of the University of Notre Dame. A rudimentary form of this work appeared in a book of essays edited by Paul Bradshaw and Bryan Spinks, and their ability to see the merits of this idea, and to encourage its expansion, was an enormous help to me.[3]

My students at Westcott House have been exceedingly patient and cheerful in the face of a certain amount of neglect, and my teaching colleagues, both in the House and in the Cambridge Theological Federation, have made generous allowances for a degree of distractedness that I have brought to my work in the past several months. I am especially grateful to the Reverend Michael Roberts, Principal of Westcott House; and to the Right Reverend Rupert Hoare, his predecessor, for their support and for taking on the extra work that my sabbatical leave made inevitable. David Cornick, Director of the Cheshunt Foundation and Director of Studies at Westminster College, has read and commented on parts of this manuscript, and as always, I stand in admiration of his penetrating and creative insights.

In March and April 1993 I spent sabbatical time working on this project at the Candler School of Theology and was given warm hospitality and a wealth of practical help by the Mission Resource Center of The United Methodist Church. To the Center staff—and especially to Allan Kirton, Connie Nelson-Daniel, and Judy Loeher—I offer my grateful thanks. Ulrike Guthrie, my editor at Abingdon Press, has worked her usual wonders with this manuscript, and has the gift of making authors feel valued and appreciated.

To check all the tiny details of a book such as this takes many hours of patient labor, and much of this work was done by my research assistant Jane Leach, who often took time for this at the expense of her own doctoral studies. Her friendship and good humor throughout this process helped to keep me on track whenever derailment was threatened. Alan Boyd of Wesley House initiated me into the mysteries of a new computer system, rushed to my rescue on numerous occasions, and never once suggested that I might be a bit stupid in my approach to the world of information processing. And as always there is a special "thank you" for the many, many others, who must necessarily go unnamed, who have offered bibliographical suggestions along the way. Of course, any errors of fact or interpretation that remain in the book are my responsibility alone.

The birth pangs of any book are as difficult for those who share their lives with the author as for anyone else, and so to all my family and friends I offer both apology and thanks—apology for the varying degrees of irritability they were obliged to endure, and thanks for the tireless support they offered nevertheless! To Kenneth Cracknell especially are both these words addressed. He has been a patient friend, a generous colleague, and a joyous companion, and his encouragement and confidence in my work was unflagging. His presence is on every page of this book, and it is to him that it is dedicated.

Susan J. White
Cambridge, England

RELIGION IN AN AGE OF TECHNOLOGY

I have felt for His Wounds
in nozzles and containers.
I have wondered for the automatic devices.
I have tested inane patterns
without prejudice.
I have been on my guard
not to condemn the unfamiliar.
For it is easy to miss Him
at the turning of civilization.[1]

In "A, a, a, Domine Deus," Welsh poet and engraver David Jones describes his own relentless search for God and, in so doing, articulates the situation faced by any religious person in a technological age. But despite his dispassionate searching, Jones ultimately finds "the glazed work unrefined and the terrible crystal a stage-paste." The search for God among the "nozzles" and "automatic devices" of the modern technological world has taken him nowhere.

The task of assessing the various ways in which technology affects the religious lives of contemporary people is a complex and difficult one. Christian believers are challenged to work out their ethics and their spirituality in the face of the technologized horror of Hiroshima, Chernobyl, and Bhopal. They are forced to discover what it means to be the church when the touch of one button on the remote control brings them images of Christians killing one another in Bosnia and Belfast and the touch of another button brings them megaservices in the Crystal Cathedral or in Vatican Square. They are expected to find answers to the question, Who is Jesus Christ? for the millions of young people whose primary faithfulness is to highly technologized alternative realities such as Dungeons and Dragons and Heavy Metal video.

But certainly it is not only the various kinds of technological hardware that present challenges to responsible and faithful Christian living. There is also the larger set of values that technology calls forth and legitimates, the social and psychological "world" that technology creates. As long ago as the 1860s, poet Matthew Arnold could speak of:

> This strange disease of modern life
> With its sick hurry, its divided aims,
> Its heads o'ertaxed, its palsied hearts.[2]

And this "strange disease" has, in the late-twentieth century reached epidemic proportions. We have a sense of being moved forward at ever-accelerating pace and in directions that seem to be out of our control. Most observers of contemporary culture—not only poets, but also sociologists, ethicists, human geographers, and psychologists—describe technology and technological modes of procedure as our human "habitat," as our "environment."[3] It is not simply that most of us in the late-twentieth century rely heavily on technological ways and means of doing things in our daily life, but also that a technological worldview has pervaded society as a whole. As sociologist Peter Berger writes:

> Everyday life in just about every one of its sectors is ongoingly bombarded, not only with material objects and processes derived from technological production, but with clusters of consciousness originating within the latter . . . [which serve] as contributions to an overarching symbolic universe peculiar to modernity.[4]

This highlights one of the primary obstacles to making an assessment of the ways in which technology is affecting our religious lives: it is difficult, if not impossible, to stand *outside* it. It has become the matrix of our ordinary living. We are awakened in the morning to the sound of the radio newscast, drive to work through a system of automated traffic signals, spend the next eight hours in a computer-ized office (linked through various networks to other such offices). Then we return home to food prepared in a microwave oven; entertain ourselves with television, videotapes, and digitalized music; set the electronic burglar-alarm system; and go to bed. And if we have had contact during the day with the medical profession, the insurance or banking industries, or the airlines, our sense of dependence on technological artifacts and processes dramatically increases. We place a high degree of *trust* in these things and in the sociotechnical systems that produce and support them. To be a contemporary human being is to be caught up in the web technology has set for us. And it is this that makes it so difficult to get the distance required for an unprejudiced evaluation of the specific ways in which technology affects our thinking about God, our believing in God, and our walking with God.

Of course, the presence of technology itself is nothing new. Theologian Paul Tillich argues that technology, along with language, is a fundamental dimension of the human person in every age, one of the essential preconditions for our self-actualization.[5] *Homo sapiens* is also *homo faber*, and questions surrounding the role of technology in human life are as old as philosophy itself.[6] Indeed, a whole category of religious narratives can be read as seeking to explicate this relationship. Tillich claims:

> The ambiguity of freedom and limitation in technical production is powerfully expressed in myths and legends. It underlies the biblical story of the tree of knowledge from which Adam eats against the will of the gods and in the Greek myth of Prometheus, who brings fire to men, also against the gods' will. Perhaps the story of the Tower of Babel, telling of man's desire to be united under a symbol in which his own finitude is overcome and the divine sphere reached, is nearest to our own situation.[7]

To a certain extent, then, men and women in every age have had to integrate technology into their personal and communal perspective, and to manage the social, moral, and intellectual anxieties that the relationship with technology occasions. Every age, then, is truly an "Age of Technology."

While the presence of technology is not new, what *is* new to Western society on the eve of the twenty-first century is the global-

15

ized, ideological pervasiveness of patterns of technical production, technological devices, and ways of thinking. "Technology," says ethicist Jacques Ellul, "is not content with *being*, or in our world, with being the *principal* or *determining factor*. Technology has become a system."[8] As a result, defining technology and the technological system and isolating its essential characteristics and its psychosocial effects have been matters of serious concern both for sociologists and philosophers of science for nearly fifty years.

WHAT IS TECHNOLOGY?

Most social analysts agree that technology can be defined on at least three distinct, but interpenetrating, levels:

I.   The term *technology* refers to the artifacts resulting from a process of manufacturing. This can be anything from a simple tool to a complex information-management system.[9] Anything that by its existence extends the range of human capabilities beyond its natural limitations falls within this definition.

II.   *Technology* also refers to the constellation of processes and structures by which such artifacts come into being. Assembly lines, automation, microprocessing, and robotics are included within this definition, as well as the kinds of human skills, techniques, and knowledge needed to accomplish the tasks related to manufacture.

III.   The term *technology* also is applied to the larger set of attitudes and presuppositions that support and advance the technological enterprise. This conceptual framework underlies the sense of a pervasive "technoculture."

Most often in ordinary discourse, these three separate definitions are taken together to refer to a sociotechnical system in which hardware, technique, and a particular ideological frame of reference combine to aid in the pursuit of essentially pragmatic ends, generally associated with the augmentation of human capabilities.[10]

Telling the story of technology and its impact on human life has become a significant area of academic interest. Begun in the 1940s and 1950s by scholars such as Lynn White Jr. and Melvin Kranzberg, the historical, sociological, and philosophical study of artifacts and processes of technology has resulted in a rich and fascinating body of literature that has made an enormous contribution to our understanding of the changing shape of society over time. Fierce debates continue to be conducted about the nature of technology, its relative autonomy, its relationship to progress and human ecology, and its future direction. These debates are not so much the result of minor differences in interpretation, but are fueled by fundamental disagreements about the causes and effects of technological development. Is technological change in essence evolutionary or revolutionary? Can technology be understood as a "thing" or only as a number of separate and independent "things"? Is technology in any sense autonomous, with its own momentum and direction, or do human beings and human systems still maintain some control over it? Does technological development always and only happen in response to economic necessity? Can we include in one single conceptual framework the diverse manifestations of the technological impulse?

Many people with an academic and professional interest in religion have been paying careful attention to the process of clarifying and refining these kinds of questions. In addition, as ethicists, psychologists and sociologists of religion, and systematic theologians have brought their own specialized concerns into the larger conversation, they have begun to ascertain some of the direct connections between technology and the religious life. Although this discussion has been uneven (both in scope and quality), theologians have begun to argue that there are particular features of the world technology has built and is building that have special significance for the religious quest.

RELIGION AND TECHNOLOGY IN DIALOGUE

Although, as Tillich points out, religion has been engaged in a dialogue with technology since the discovery of fire, it was not until the Middle Ages that a body of more detailed responses by Christian theologians to the presence and influence of technology can be identified. But there was by no means a uniform view. The writer of the *Nuremberg Chronicle* in 1398 argues that the "wheeled engines performing strange tasks and shows and follies" of medieval machinery "come directly from the Devil." At the same time, illuminated manuscripts from the thirteenth to the fifteenth century show God with calipers and compasses measuring out the celestial spheres, and adjusting the lifespan of Hezekiah in 2 Kings 20 by resetting an elaborate mechanical clock. While the Virtues, and especially Temperance, were represented by clocks and mills,[11] the earliest image of the printing press in the fifteenth century shows a room full of people operating presses, each of whom is being hindered in his work by a skeleton, the symbol of impending death and decay.[12] (By the turn of the sixteenth century, similar depictions of presses being operated have angels standing at the edges of the scene.) This kind of dance between delight and dread, which is manifested in the medieval iconographic record, has marked religion's attitude to technology from the very beginning, and certainly describes the contemporary discussion as well.

For most of human history, the pace of this dance was fairly steady, but it accelerated markedly as the West began to assess the impact of the ninteenth-century Industrial Revolution on various aspects of life, including the spiritual and religious life. During this period the rise of Protestant evangelicalism, Oxford and Cambridge Movement romanticism, Christian socialism, and Vatican Council I absolutism can all be seen as directly linked to the social and psychological upheaval that accompanied the burgeoning of industrial technology.[13] It was in the nineteenth century that the power of technology was first identified, the potential of technology was first appreciated, and the problems associated with technology were first experienced by wide segments of the population. In large measure, the various attitudes of religious people today toward technology can be traced directly to these nineteenth-century reactions to the newly industrialized world.

In the late-twentieth century much of the work toward a definition of the relationship between religion and technology has been part of a larger search for an understanding of the nature of modernity. There is a startling array of descriptions for the social situation in which people in the late-twentieth-century West are embedded. There are those that highlight a guiding principle of organization, such as "technocracy," and "consumer society." There are those that illuminate a particular mode of social interaction: "information society," and "transpersonal society." And there are also those that imply a situation of radical discontinuity with the past and that suggest that the previous age has passed away, for example "post-Modernity,"[14] "postcapitalism," and "postindustrialism." Each of these, however, highlights a decisive shift not only in technological hardware, production techniques, and processes, but also in basic human values and attitudes.

To most observers, the search for the origins of modernity leads, almost inevitably, to the machine, and the culture that grew up around the machine has been given serious and sustained attention both by theologians and by historians and philosophers of technology.[15] Beginning with the rise of industrialism in the eighteenth and nineteenth centuries, the machine quickly became both the principal method of production and the principal metaphor for the progressive perfectibility of humankind. But it was something even more than that. As Lewis Mumford says:

> The machine was the substitute for . . . the Christian ideals of grace and redemption. The machine came forth as the new demi-urge that was to create a new heaven and a new earth: or at least, as a new Moses, that was to lead the barbarous humanity into the Promised Land.[16]

This way of talking about machine technology is not surprising. By the turn of the twentieth century the increasing mastery of nature by the machine had swelled food production, extended the life span, eliminated various diseases, improved the standard of living, and expanded communications and mobility. Routinely, industrial technology began to be approached with a sort of religious awe. Artist Francis Picaba, who visited America with his friend Marcel Duchamp in 1917, remarked: "The machine has become more than a mere adjunct of human life. It is really a part of human life—perhaps the very soul."[17]

The lifeblood of the machine-dominated culture was the concept of productivity, the quest for which was itself undertaken with a genuinely religious zeal. As early as 1853, an English visitor to America concluded:

the real secret of American productivity is that American society is imbued, through and through, with the desirability, the rightness, the morality of production. Men serve God in America, in all seriousness and sincerity, through striving for economic efficiency.[18]

Efficiency, productivity, and progress became the goals in almost every department of life, and were practically embodied in the labor-organization concept called Taylorism. In 1911, Frederick W. Taylor's *Principles of Scientific Management* proposed "a system of production involving both men and machines that would be as efficient as a single well-oiled machine."[19] Detailed work schedules, flowcharts, and time-and-motion studies guided the Taylor workplace, and his books and lectures spread his ideas throughout the United States. The assembly line, the mechanical device, and the inventor became quasi-religious symbols of the new America. One early-nineteenth-century enthusiast writes:

Such is the factory system replete with prodigies in mechanics and political economy, which promises, in its future growth, to become the great minister of civilization to the terraqueous globe, enabling this country, as its heart, to diffuse along with its commerce, the life-blood of science and religion to myriads of people still lying "in the region and shadow of death."[20]

Most of those involved in the dialogue between religion and technology agree that a belief in progress, productivity, and efficiency continues to be an aspect of the psychosocial world which the machine and machine production created, and within which religious people operate. But during the past 50 years both technological hardware and technological ways of thinking have moved into new relationships with society, relationships which are at once more subtle and more pervasive, more ambiguous and more potent than was the case in the mechanical-industrial past. Rapid technological innovation has presented new challenges to the various subdisciplines of religious studies as each new technology "rearranges our perceptual world, and subtly redefines our relationship to our environment."[21]

Many theologians are convinced that the pervasiveness of a technoculture has shaken the very foundations of classical Christianity: tradition, authority, certainty, hegemony. Beginning with the rise of seventeenth-century Enlightenment Rationalism, and paralleling the growth of industrialization, the cohesive set of trusted symbols by which Christianity had previously been defined and expressed began to collapse and traditional structures of authority began to weaken as certainty came to be equated with provability, materiality, and universality.[22] It began to be expected that power should be legitimized by popular assent.[23] It began to be known that a plurality of choices was available, and that any of these choices could be taken up by independent human agents without coercion or constraint. As society has become increasingly technologized, a number of these trends have been reinforced: the need for assent to authority, the emphasis on the "self," and the necessity of a rational validation of truth.[24] But at the same time, other post-Enlightenment trends have been called into question by the pervasiveness of technology, and particularly the notion that there can be any form of universal or timeless truth and that independent choice is always possible. In other words, a world dominated by technology tends to *increase* our sense of the alternative futures available to us, but at the same time it tends to *decrease* our sense of control over and autonomy within those futures.

This sort of analysis has been of particular concern to ethicists, who see it as part of the matrix within which moral decisions are undertaken. Some, such as Jacques Ellul, would go as far as to say that technology is now the absolute condition for all moral decision making. But since technology is completely out of our control, Ellul argues, our moral selves are now completely out of control as well.[25] The only possibility of living as faithful Christian believers is to reject totally the world technology has made. Many contemporary religious novelists and poets reinforce this sense of hopelessness about our ethical situation. R. S. Thomas, one of the most resolute of Welsh poets, says:

> "The body is mine and the soul is mine"
> says the machine. "I am the dark source
> where good is indistinguishable
> from evil. I fill my tanks up

and there is war. I empty them
and there is not peace. I am the sound,
not of the world breathing, but
of the catch in the world's breath."[26]

Others are less pessimistic. Jürgen Moltmann, with his political
theology rooted in the concept of a distinctively Christian hope, says:

If it is hope that maintains and upholds faith and keeps it moving
on, if it is hope that draws the believer into the life of love, then it
will also be hope that is the mobilizing and driving force of faith's
thinking, of its knowledge of, and reflections on, human nature,
history and society.[27]

For others, such as Ian Barbour, technology remains ambiguous,
and it is only as we are caught up in the interplay of self and society
that we can determine how technology and morality actually interact. Technology has indeed set up a new range of moral problems,
but it has also set up a new range of moral solutions; for each
technological challenge there is a technological response, which at
the same time embodies Christian principles.[28]

If the moral ground has been shaken by the pervasiveness of
technology, the sense of tradition has been shaken as well.

M. Francis Mannion points out that "the electronic media reduce
public life, education, art, and history," which are the traditional
bearers of tradition "to show business and entertainment."[29] In this
way, Mannion claims, these things are trivialized, and thereby lose
"their moral seriousness and their integral value as autonomous
agents of social edification."[30] This sort of trivialization of the bearers
of sociocultural tradition extends to the bearers of religious tradition
as well. One prominent theologian describes the current situation as
one in which increasing numbers of people regard all religions as
possible sources of symbols to be used eclectically in articulating,
clarifying, and organizing the experience of the inner self.[31]

Since the maintaining of tradition also depends upon a meaning-
ful continuity of past and present, tradition also breaks down with
the increasing fragmentation of time and experience, which technological society intensifies. "Work time" is clearly demarcated from
"free time," and "religious time" is separated from "secular time."

Childhood, adolescence, maturity, and old age are each given their own set of symbolic associations and their own particular technological framework.[32]

Added to this is an overarching sense of uncertainty, the sense that as much as one tries to anticipate the future course of events, the direction in which technological development is taking the world remains unpredictable. Because we cannot plan decisively for a future, but can only plot out "alternative futures," our sense of temporal dislocation is increased—past, present, and future are not linked by cause and effect in the same way that they were. The ambiguity of this situation is highlighted by social analyst E. L. Trist, who argues that in a technological society an increased need for planning is necessarily accompanied by an increased inability to plan: "The greater the degree of change, the greater the need for planning, otherwise precedents of the past could guide the future; but the greater the degree of uncertainty, the greater the likelihood that plans right today will be wrong tomorrow." Because of this kind of dilemma, Trist concludes by confessing that "I find I cannot re-capture that sense of solid earth I once took for granted."[33] This kind of experience has further consequences for the maintaining of structures (such as religion) that depend to a large extent on tradition and continuity.

CONTEMPORARY THEOLOGIANS RESPOND TO TECHNOLOGY

In all of this, theologians have tended to adopt one of three distinct positions with regard to technology. Some are utterly pessimistic about technology. It is a threat to any sort of authentic human life, and especially to the religious and spiritual life. As it imposes its own criteria on the world and conforms all human existence to those criteria, technology enslaves and dehumanizes every person it encounters. We have already mentioned Jacques Ellul, perhaps the most articulate of the technopessimists, whose books *The Technological Society*,[34] *The Technological System*,[35] and *The Technological Bluff*[36] present a vision of a technological apparatus, which is pervasive, autonomous, and self-determining. Although he believes that a biblically based Christian ethics can provide a benchmark for judging the effects of technology, Ellul sees little hope for escaping the negative effects of technology on individuals and society. Because technology is impersonal, Ellul and the other pessimists contend, it eats away at personality; because technology is autonomous, materialistic, and commercial, it feeds on the perpetual manufacture of human needs and desires; because technology is deterministic, it is fueled by the disempowerment of individuals.

As one would expect, technology has powerful effects on the religious life for the pessimists. Its imperialistic domination of human purposes undermines the necessary self-determination that individuals need for true religious commitment.[37] The commercial and materialist elements of technologized living erode our sense of the sacred. The fragmentation of experience and superficiality that technology demands keeps us from finding depth of meaning, and the manipulation of dependency and risk that technology relies upon distracts us from the spiritual sources of assurance. All in all, the essential elements of an age of technology are antithetical to the religious life. In addition, for the hardcore pessimists like Ellul, there is nothing we can do to resist its effects.

Other theologians are more optimistic about the relationship between technology and the spiritual quest. Technology has increased our ability to feed and clothe the earth's inhabitants, it has reduced sickness and increased the human life span, and in so doing has released us to focus on spiritual matters more intentionally. In addition, technology has increased the levels of human freedom and autonomy, so that the choice of a religious path is now more likely to be independent and unconstrained rather than coerced. We can, through improved communication, assess the degree and kind of human want anywhere on the globe and, through improved transportation, we can be the answer to prayer for the relieving of that human want. Through technology workers will "find relief from otherwise intolerable conditions through higher wages, more leisure, better recreation,"[38] and can thus be more receptive to the gospel. Technology for the optimists is not an autonomous force, out of our direct control, but a tool for the improvement of human living, about which we make independent choices every day. Technology is a part of the Christian future, and it will be through technology that the evangelization of the whole world will at last be accomplished.

In recent years a third view of technology, which attempts to negotiate a path between extreme optimism and extreme pessimism, has begun to emerge. Articulated most recently by ethicist Ian Barbour, this view might be called *contextualism*.[39] For the contextualists, both the religious life and technology are part of the fabric of human existence, and they mutually influence each other (or have the potential to do so) at a variety of points. As Barbour says:

> Technology influences human life but is itself part of a cultural system; it is an instrument of social power serving the purposes of those who control it. It does systematically impose distinctive forms on all areas of life, but these can be modified through political processes.[40]

In other words, although technology is a powerful force, it can be ordered and redirected through the application of human will and commitment. Technology bears within it both the seeds of human destruction and the seeds of human transformation. It has the potential to deepen and enrich the religious life, or to weaken and degrade it. Which of these ultimately will be the case is a matter of individual and communal choice.

CONCLUSION

The history, philosophy, and social impact of technology have been of real interest to those working in a number of theological disciplines. But because there is a wide diversity in interpretations of technology, there is an equally wide diversity in interpretations of its relationship to Christian belief and practice. In many ways, the place of technology in the making of an environment for Christianity remains ambiguous, and it is also increasingly clear that different technologies have different effects on individuals and societies. The electronic media alters our sense of time and place, the technology of warfare increases our existential dread, biotechnics shifts the balance of power in matters of life and death, manufacturing technology increases our sense of the fragmentation of experience, information technology pushes us out into a globalized network of interconnections.[41] Issues of trust and doubt, freedom and constraint, certainty and uncertainty, individual and collective, stability and change arise over and over again in the discussion. The eloquent pessimists and the eloquent optimists about the future of technology continue to debate these matters, and are now being joined by those who see the very ambiguity of technology as its essential feature.

Perhaps the search for God among the "nozzles and containers" of technological society is indeed doomed to failure. Perhaps, however, with a creative cross-fertilization of insights from the various theological disciplines, some sense of how we might be authentically Christian in the presence of technology can be gained. So far, ethicists and sociologists of religion have borne the weight of the work, with systematic theologians making some significant contributions here and there. But because being authentically Christian is not only a matter of belief and morality, but is also a matter of what might be called the "practice of religion" (including symbolic and ritual action, the maintaining of traditions, and personal and corporate piety), members of all theological disciplines must begin to share in the discussion. If those specifically concerned with the study of Christian worship can begin to ask themselves how the technological matrix functions and has functioned as a context for the public prayer of the people of God, the discussion of the relationship between religion and technology will surely be deepened, enriched, and expanded.

CHAPTER
T W O

TECHNOLOGY AS A CHALLENGE FOR THE STUDY OF CHRISTIAN WORSHIP

As we have seen, many theologians, ethicists, and sociologists of religion are beginning to view technology as primary shaper of the context within which contemporary people search for a relationship with God, and are increasingly including technology as a dialogue partner in the process of "faith seeking understanding." Therefore, the questions raised by technological hardware, processes, and ways of thinking are gradually becoming clearer in such fields of inquiry as ethics and pastoral theology.[1] But what specific kinds of questions does technology raise for those who study and participate in the worship of the church?

An inspection of the literature in the history, theology, and practice of Christian public prayer might seem to suggest that technology (and, by extension, the technologized, twentieth-century human) raises almost no questions at all for worship and worshipers, that it falls completely outside the field of attention. In a few cases, this is the result of a sharp intellectual division between sacred and secular spheres. Technology and its consequences are concerns of the world; Christian worship and its consequences, concerns of the churches. And without a common boundary, there is no real point of encounter at which dialogue might take place. But while this kind of thinking affects some bands on the liturgical spectrum,[2] it is not particularly widespread and does not account for the more generalized innocence of the "technological matrix" that the study of Christian worship, both past and present, has displayed.

So why have those concerned with the worship of the church given so little attention to the impact of technology? At least part of the answer lies in the way in which worship as an academic discipline has been defined and developed. For much of its history,[3] "liturgiology" was confined to the examination and interpretation of specific liturgical texts; and whether these texts were ancient or modern, the method of analysis and interpretation has been the same. Prayers and rubrics are subjected to careful exegesis, internal changes are catalogued, and lines of influence are drawn between and among the various rites and families of rites. For those working on ancient, patristic, and early-medieval sources (and such people have always been viewed as the academic elite of the liturgy world), the quest for the "Ur-text" of a given form of prayer has tended to dominate scholarly attention: What was the original form of words Jesus used at the Last Supper? What was the most ancient text of the liturgy of St. Mark or St. Basil? What was the most primitive shape of the epiclesis or institution narrative of the Christian year?[4] This has meant that the handmaidens of the study of liturgy have traditionally been philology, canon law, and historiography rather than theology, sociology, or human geography.

Those who have been involved with the revision of worship materials for all denominations during the past thirty years have been heavily influenced by this approach to liturgical studies, and the resulting official liturgies strongly reflect this. The claim to "antiquity" has been seen as a guarantee that a rite or text is adequate and appropriate for faithful Christian people in any age. The widespread use of the liturgical texts attributed to Hippolytus of Rome (ca. 215 C.E.) in the revisions of the Eucharist and Baptism is one powerful example of this approach, but other ancient texts have also been culled for liturgical material to be used in modern prayer-writing. This practice is rarely questioned. For instance, in *Eucharist: Symbol of Transformation*, William Crockett can simply take for granted this process of liturgical archaeology when he says:

> Liturgical research in the present century has given us a clearer picture of the shape and development of the early liturgy and of the origin and development of the Eucharistic Prayer.... These

results of liturgical research together with the movement of liturgical renewal have led to several major projects of liturgical revision on the part of a number of western Churches.[5]

Crockett goes on to cite examples of this historicist mode of liturgical revision, beginning with Roman Catholics, and followed by Anglicans, Lutherans, Methodists, and the United Church of Canada. (To this list must now be added American Presbyterians, and their recent series of *Supplemental Liturgical Resources,* which culminated in the 1993 *Book of Common Worship.*) He then comments that "all of these revisions are marked by a return to the basic shape of the early eucharistic liturgy and by a recovery of the tradition of the Eucharistic Prayer."[6] A similar process has occurred in the contemporary revisions of the rites of initiation, daily prayer, reconciliation, and to a lesser extent, the Christian calendar and the marriage and funeral services.

It is true that a number of things that scholars had taken for granted about the ancient liturgical sources are now beginning to be called into question. Some researchers, like Paul Bradshaw, have suggested that we can no longer be as certain of the authenticity, antiquity, and authority of these ancient texts as we might be, or as confident about their interrelationships and development. But Bradshaw also expresses concern over the use of antique prayers in a modern context, and accuses those involved in liturgical revision of failing to use due caution in their use of historical resources:

> They have simply plundered what they wanted to fit the picture of the early Church they were attempting to paint, without asking themselves why it ever came to be there in the first place, and what this might have to say about its value as historical evidence.[7]

Bradshaw asks his liturgist colleagues to "avoid the practice of simply abstracting pieces without reference to their context—what one might call the 'hit and run' approach to historical sources."[8] But to date, few have heeded his warnings.

With such high professional investment in the value of ancient liturgical forms, and in the ability of ancient forms to meet contemporary euchological and spiritual needs, it is little wonder that the wider human contexts within which such prayers operate has had such a low profile. If we want prayers to be fully and easily *transfer-*

able from one social, cultural, economic, theological situation to another, then they must be seen to be fully and easily *detachable* from that situation. Only if we regard a text or rite as an autonomous, self-contained entity can we shift it from one context to another without a significant change in or deformation of its meaning. In other words, in order to treat historic texts as we have done in the process of contemporary liturgical revision, we have had to ignore, to a certain extent, their deep interconnectedness with (and dependence upon) their own world.

Technology is a part of the "world" of public prayer: as much a part of the world of ancient, medieval, and Reformation public prayer as it is of the world of modern public prayer. But the coalition between historicism and modern liturgical revision and the resulting demand that rites and texts "stand on their own two feet" has encouraged the devaluation of the technological matrix (along with the social, economic, cultural, and political matrices) within which liturgy operates.[9]

But of course the study of worship has not been solely historicist in its outlook and method, and the renewal of worship has not been solely committed to the recapitulation of ancient formulas. There has been a second, and equally powerful, trend in the field, and this has also had an impact on our approach to questions of technology. This second trend is grounded on an important insight—namely, that the phenomenon we call Christian worship is a subset of human religious behavior in general, and that anthropological studies of ritual can shed some light on the deep structures of our Christian ways of worshiping God. And so, since about the middle of this century, the academic study of the church's liturgy has also been heavily influenced by insights from the human sciences[10] and particularly from the field of ritual studies. The work of socioanthropologists such as Victor Turner, Claude Lévi-Strauss, Arnold van Gennep, and Mary Douglas has had an enormous impact on the thinking of liturgists, and whole areas of the theology and practice of worship have been revised on the basis of that work.[11]

While this dependence on ritual studies has been enormously valuable in giving us a sense of the interconnectedness of all human religious behavior, of which Christian liturgy is a part, it has been generally detrimental to a scholarly interest in the impact of technology on our worship. This is because the *type* of ritual-studies research that has been appropriated by liturgists has been largely "primitivist" in character. Preliterate people from Africa, tribal groups in remote parts of Asia and Indonesia, and hunter-gatherers in the Arctic have been the models which guided the understanding of students of Christian worship in this area.[12] Gradually, our expectations about what is normative for Christian religious ritual have been shaped by what we know about the religious ritual of those for whom the impact of a technological society is slight. With regard to rites of initiation, for example, one liturgist confidently says:

> A place to begin a study of baptism is with the recognition that any society needs to initiate new members into it. Some societies do this better than others, and it is obvious that initiation rites reach their maximal expressions in societies which are relatively stable and where change is bound up with biological processes and meteorological rhythms.[13]

Because this sense of the normativeness of primitive religious experience is so prevalent, Victor Turner's definition of worship has become something of a standard: "prescribed formal behavior for occasions *not given over to technological routine.*"[14]

If the "modern technological person" is discussed at all in the current climate, he or she tends to be discussed as a liturgical or ritual "problem." Many liturgists speak about a debilitating fragmentation of experience in contemporary society, in which work, home, religion, and leisure are compartmentalized rather than integrated. As Turner says, "The clear division between work and leisure which modern industry has produced has affected all symbolic genres, from ritual to games to literature."[15]

As we have seen, many theologians would subscribe, at least implicitly, to this idea that modern technology and technological ways of thinking are unalterably opposed to the nature of the religious quest, and that the impact of technology is something to be fought against. Clearly, the impact of a ritual-studies approach to liturgy has exacerbated this feeling with regard to Christian common prayer.

Because of this attitude, the most usual way of posing the question that technology raises for worship is, How can Christian ritual be so forged as to be an effective weapon in the battle against the forces of technologized modernity? Allied to this is the sense that the pervasiveness of a technological worldview has seriously eroded the ability of modern men and women to ritualize their religious experiences, and that the role of the liturgist is, in part, to "re-educate" a whole generation of Christian believers into more "primitive" ways of being human.[16]

One final trend in the study of liturgy deserves mention as we assess the causes for a lack of scholarly interest in the impact of technology on Christian worship. Inculturation[17] has become an increasingly important concept within a whole range of theological disciplines, including doctrine, ethics, and missiology. Although the *practice* of inculturation is as old as the Christian church itself, the *principles* of inculturation only began to be refined and systematized by Roman Catholics during the period of theological fecundity immediately preceding Vatican II.[18] In the *Constitution on the Sacred Liturgy* (III:37-40), there was an effort to apply these principles to the revision of liturgical rites. Having stated that the Church "respects and fosters the spiritual adornments and gifts of the various races and peoples," the document goes on to say that anything that is "not indissolubly bound up with superstition and error" is to be approached with sympathy and, if possible, to be preserved intact.[19] Because of this, "Provided that the substantial unity of the Roman rite is maintained, the revision of liturgical books should allow for legitimate variations and adaptations to different groups, regions, and peoples, especially in mission lands."[20]

Thus, the primary concern during the early days of thinking about liturgical inculturation was with the ways in which Western rites could be adjusted or augmented to suit the spiritual and religious needs of non-Western cultures.[21] (In the beginning the practical consequences of this work were mainly confined to an encouragement of the "liturgical arts": vestments, music and dance, and the plastic arts.[22]) Many liturgists were also deeply concerned with matters of canon law, ecclesiastical authority, and with defining the legitimate limits of deviation from the officially promulgated rites.

As practical and theological questions about the inculturation of Christian worship were taken up by Protestants of various denominations and by national and international councils of churches,[23] attention shifted away from concern with the adaptation of official rites. But primary emphasis continued to be placed upon non-Western cultures, and the ways in which worship might be adapted to support Christian missions. In addition, highly influential books such as Vincent Donovan's *Christianity Rediscovered: An Epistle from the Masai*,[24] and more recently David Bosch's *Transforming Mission: Paradigm Shifts in Theology of Mission*[25] have encouraged us to see that inculturation is not a one-way process by which some "normative" (i.e., Western) liturgical form is allowed to be changed to accommodate the needs of a different culture. True inculturation recognizes that those outside Western technological society have deep liturgical insights to offer, which must be on equal footing in the dialogue with Western liturgical forms.

The idea that traditional forms of Christian worship might actually need to be "indigenized" to the specific and cultural and religious needs of late-twentieth-century Western industrialized people is only recently beginning to be discussed. Some commentators have remarked upon the lack of technological imagery and metaphors in prayers and hymns, and "Few have made the attempt to harness urban and industrial concepts to the purposes of proclaiming or revealing God's wonders. Richard Jones's [hymn] 'God of concrete, God of steel' has painfully few imitators."[26]

There is the growing recognition that most traditional liturgical images are rooted in pastoral and preindustrial life and that images from the world of technology and industry, if they have appeared at all in common prayer, have generally pointed us to something in urgent need of redemption. God communicates self through sheep and shepherds, green rolling hills and starry skies, springtime and harvest; and evil lurks on urban streets and in "dark satanic mills."[27]

Those searching for appropriate historical models for developing a positive relationship between liturgy and technology have had to look long and hard. The most significant historical example of a well-integrated technological-liturgical system can be found in the social theory of Claude Henri de Saint-Simon (1760–1825), a post-Revolutionary French philosopher who is called the "father of technocracy." Having divided the population into three categories (laborers and administrators, scientists and inventors, and artists and religious leaders) Saint-Simon proposed a society that would be a "scientific-industrial association" whose goal would be "the highest productive effort to conquer nature and to achieve the greatest possible benefits for all."[28] In the religion of Saint-Simon, collective worship would be so designed as to overcome individualism and thus be an effective support to the collaboration needed for industrial production.[29] The Saint-Simonian priest was to ensure that worship aided in the breakdown of the old class system and redistributed wealth, and the Saint-Simonian worshiper was to find in the liturgy a mirror of the perfect technocracy.[30] This "would bring a new religion of collective worship to the people that would overcome individual egoism." But liturgists have yet to find ways of interpreting Saint-Simonian worship, and of applying insights in this area to liturgical questions in the late-twentieth century.

Because this sort of investigation is in its very earliest stages, the theological and practical guidelines for contextualizing the liturgy within a technologically sophisticated culture have yet to be developed. For the most part, the emphasis on inculturation in recent liturgical studies has discouraged rather than encouraged an interest in assessing the impact of technology on Christian worship and worshipers. And many continue to subscribe (implicitly or explicitly) to the primitivist ideal, encouraged both by ritual studies and by recent trends in the theology of inculturation—that worship in the non-Western, preliterate, tribal world is innately superior to our own, and that unless we return to our "natural" (i.e. nontechnological) state we will never find our worship truly satisfying.

But for a number of reasons, not everyone will be comfortable with this sort of analysis. For some it will seem excessively simplistic; for others, excessively negative. If inculturation and contextualization have taught us anything, it is that we must look very carefully at human ritual subjects as we find them and not as we would wish them to be, and that it is unlikely that we can strip away the layers of civilization and modernity and uncover the naked human subject.[31] Indeed, most sociologists agree that it is impossible to turn back the clock in order to create a psychosocial Garden of Eden.

> Contemporary society cannot divest itself of its technological structures. . . . If we are "stuck with" technology and bureaucracy we are also "stuck with" those structures of consciousness that are intrinsic to those processes. Put differently, there are those packages [of consciousness] that cannot be taken apart.[32]

34

Presuming that this is true, I would like to suggest that there are at least three more "neutral" questions that can and should be addressed to the technological situation by those with interest in Christian worship. These questions are directly linked to the three "definitions" of technology we have offered above.[33]

The first is, in essence, a question of "hardware": What have been the actual points of intersection between the history of technological change and the history of liturgical change? How has technology, its artifacts and processes, been incorporated into and shifted the direction of the development of Christian worship? To answer this kind of question, we must presuppose that worship is shaped not only by ecclesiastical forces, but by forces operating in the larger social context of which it is a part. This kind of attention to the societal matrix has already had a profound effect on scholarly approaches to the Bible, historical theology, and the history of Christianity,[34] and the study of the church's liturgy must surely also operate on this level.

It must be said that historians of technology have already made some very interesting efforts toward a correlation of liturgical and technological data, seeking to understand the degree to which changes in technology can be explained as responses to changing trends in Christian worship. Two important examples provide analyses of early-medieval farming technology and labor management: Lynn White Jr. and George Ovitt both look to monastic liturgical practice, and particularly to the recitation of the daily office, as the primary stimulus to developments in medieval farming techniques and to what Ovitt calls the "secularization of labor."[35] They demonstrate that the expectation that religious communities would be economically self-sufficient could not be met by men and women who gathered regularly to say the office, and that this conflict (most often resolved in favor of the priority of reciting the office) engendered revolutionary changes in techniques for planting, ploughing, and harvesting, and also provided the occasion for experiments with a division of labor and specialization. This kind of research has enlarged our understanding of historical processes and has been of enormous benefit in the development of the history of technology as a discipline.

Clearly, the history of liturgy would also benefit from similar efforts by students of Christian worship. But this means that as we try to develop an accurate account of the history of liturgical development, as we ask why certain liturgical shifts occurred or why they occurred at a particular time or place, the technological matrix needs to be considered alongside the theological, the sociological, and the political. We must even be willing to acknowledge that in certain cases a given development in worship was more dependent on technology than on any other single factor. The points of contact between the history of technological change and the history of liturgical change can be analyzed in terms of several broad classes of technological hardware: biotechnology, information processing, sanitation, time keeping and astronomical instrumentation, and transport all have exercised influence on the shape of Christian worship and Christian worshipers in various ways and at various times. The stories of these intersections are not only of interest for their own sake, but they also help to place a discussion of the relationship between technology and worship in the modern period into perspective.

The second question that technology addresses to liturgical studies correlates with our second definition of technology as a "set of processes and structures" by which work is accomplished. In what ways have these sorts of technological processes affected the way in which those who have professional responsibility for worship do their work? Have we gradually made technological ideals, modes of procedure, and frames of reference integral to the development of denominational and congregational worship? To what degree have liturgists become "technologized"?

This would seem to be a crucial time in the history of liturgics to ask these kinds of questions. Scholars in a number of disciplines that had their origins in the last century, including psychology, linguistics, and sociology are beginning to look critically at the history of changes in the goals and methods of their own fields of endeavor. This sort of historical self-analysis is now thought to be essential to the intellectual health and well-being of any scholarly community and to the responsible advancement of a field of inquiry. Within the field of liturgical studies, there has already been some important recent work on the kinds of methodologies that characterized its formative period as an academic discipline.[36] Surely the next step in this process is to ask whether modern liturgiology is shaped as much by models derived from technology as nineteenth-century liturgiology was shaped by models derived from evolutionary theory and comparative anatomy.

But there is another, and perhaps more urgent, reason for asking to what degree the work of professional liturgists has been influenced by technological modes of procedure: such people increasingly affect the worship of ordinary Christian women and men. At the denominational level, those with liturgical expertise are employed to develop service materials, plan continuing education opportunities for clergy and laity, and oversee the management of liturgical change. Official hymnals, service books, and worship guidelines are not only proliferating, but growing in their influence and authority. And this is happening across the denominational spectrum, even among Christian groups (such as Southern Baptists, Disciples of Christ, and the United Church of Christ) who have never before relied upon officially produced and authorized worship materials. In addition, changes in the seminary training of clergy have spread the influence of academic liturgiology. Where thirty years ago only Episcopal and Roman Catholic seminaries could be expected to have a professionally trained liturgist on the faculty, now nearly every United Methodist, Presbyterian, Christian Church (Disciples of Christ), and United Church of Christ seminary has someone whose primary responsibility it is to teach the history, theology, and practice of Christian worship to those preparing for the ordained ministry. Very often these seminary teachers will hold a Ph.D. in liturgy, and no matter where this degree was taken, the intellectual framework and curriculum will have been very similar in each course of study. In this way, a common set of presuppositions about what liturgy is and should be is transmitted throughout a denomination, congregation by congregation, through the parochial clergy.

But perhaps the most important question posed by the pervasiveness of technology relates to the human person as a liturgical subject. Does the modern, technologized human being interact with worship and the worshiping community in a particular fashion? Our third definition of technology speaks of a "set of attitudes and presuppositions," or, in Berger's terms, "packages of consciousness," which are part of the framework within which the technological person operates. What happens when these packages are brought to the ritual act? If liturgical studies is, in any sense, a "human science," as well as an historical and theological one, this issue must be tackled in a rigorous and intellectually respectable way.

The impact of technology and industrialization on the human ritual subject has already attracted the scholarly attention of a small number of sociologists. In *The Rites of Rulers*, for example, Christel Lane analyzes the place of ritual in modern Soviet society. Lane's detailed and insightful descriptions of the initiation rituals of industrial workers in a state factory would seem equally as important to an understanding of the deep structures of Christian worship as the work of Victor Turner on the initiation rituals of the Ndembu tribe in Zambia.[37] English sociologist Robert Bocock has studied the relationship between Christian ritualism in the nineteenth-century industrialization of England,[38] and a number of social historians have discussed the place of worship in the Wesleys' evangelization of urban Britain.[39] But very little has been done so far to apply the insights of contemporary sociological and cultural analysis to the study of Christian worship. What kind of culture is it that we are embedded in? And how does this culture shape the person who comes to the average wedding, funeral, or Sunday service?

As we have seen, various forces at work in the development of the academic study of Christian worship have made it difficult for us to attend to the impact of technology on Christian public prayer. In the chapters that follow I shall try to establish a dialogue between worship and technology by addressing ourselves to a number of the major areas of technological influence described above. Beginning with a study of the mutual influence beween liturgy and technology on liturgical work, we shall then move on to investigate a number of case studies in the history of worship and technology. Then we shall try to sketch out the ways being a part of a technological society affects participants in Christian worship, and conclude by suggesting a framework within which a dialogue between liturgy and technology might usefully proceed.

CHAPTER
THREE

SHAPING WORSHIP IN THE TECHNOLOGICAL MODE

We tend to think too much of what the church might bring to society and too little of what society is already bringing to the church. We enthuse about what new prayers and new liturgical music might do to shape the liturgical assembly, overlooking the fact that culture has gotten there before us, unconsciously shaping the attitudes and the language of both the experts and the particpants.[1]

As we saw in the previous chapter, certain characteristics of the academic study of Christian worship have made it difficult for liturgists to address technology directly as an object of intellectual inquiry. But this is not to say that the work of liturgists has not been deeply affected by technological artifacts and processes. Those responsible for the production of service materials, for the training of ordained ministers, for the advancement of academic research, and for the staffing of support and consultancy structures within denominations all find their work increasingly, if subtly, "technologized" in ways that merit attention and evaluation. In the pages that follow, we shall look at two specific ways in which the working life of professional liturgists has been influenced by technology. The first relates to what we have previously described as technological "hardware," the intersection between the history of a particular technology and liturgical work. The second relates to the ways in which the wider structures and processes that operate within a technological society as a whole shape the methods by which official liturgical texts are produced. Taken together, they provide some insight into the kind of power that technology exerts on liturgical work at every level. But this kind of study is not only valuable as a part of building up a picture of how a particular discipline changes over time. It is also important as a way of understanding the relationship between a body of religious professionals and the worship life of ordinary individuals and congregations.

INFORMATION PROCESSING AND THE LITURGY

The term *information processing* covers an extraordinarily wide variety of procedures, systems, and technical apparatus. From the organization of labor in the monastic scriptorium to the organization of microchips in the laptop computer, from the development of paper and mechanical printing presses to the development of television and satellite networking: all find a place in the history of information technology.[2] In the late-twentieth century, social analysts have attempted to assess the impact of the various modes of information technology, and while they may disagree about specific cases, they tend to come to a common mind with Marshall McLuhan: "Each new medium alters permanently our psychic environment, imposing on us a particular pattern of perceiving and thinking that controls us to an extent we scarcely suspect."[3] Christian worship has not been exempt from this kind of alteration, and not only to the shape of our "psychic environment" as worshipers, but also to the ways and means by which liturgy comes into being.

Most scholarship in this area has been confined to the importance of the printing press in the spread of Reformation liturgical principles.[4] But information technology has, in fact, exerted its influence over the entire history of Christian worship. Indeed, as we shall see, each of the major historical shifts in information processing corresponds to a significant point of transition of the way in which Christian liturgy has been ordered, disseminated, and received. In this section we shall follow one particular thread through the fabric of information technology, one that will lead us from the growth of a written standard for communication in the third-century church, to the organization of copyists in the public and monastic scriptoria in the sixth century, to the spread of the printing press in the fifteenth and sixteenth centuries, and on to the computer in the twentieth century.

In his *First Apology*, written around 150 C.E., the Christian teacher and theologian Justin of Rome attempted to dispel public suspicions about the activities of the increasingly influential religious movement. After discussing questions of conversion and Christology, Justin describes the celebration of the Eucharist with which he is familiar. "The president of the community," Justin explains, "gives thanks at considerable length,"[5] offering to God "prayers and thanksgivings to the best of his ability."[6] Although debates over the meaning of the phrase "to the best of his ability" (*hose dunamis auto*) have been vigorous,[7] scholarly opinion now seems to support the idea that in this early period it was expected that the central prayer of the Eucharist (at least) would be improvised by the president of the assembly.[8] Further textual support for this idea comes about sixty years later, with the so-called *Apostolic Tradition* attributed to Hippolytus.[9] Having given an example of the kind of prayer that is to be used at the Eucharist, the text continues with the words, "Let the bishop give thanks in accordance with what we have said above. It is not necessary for him to say the same words we gave above, as though striving to say them by heart, when giving thanks to God; but let each one pray according to his own ability."[10]

The evidence for a generally extemporized Christian liturgy in this early period is quite persuasive.[11] Always, however, there is the caution expressed within the texts that such praying should be "within the conventions"[12] or "soundly orthodox."[13] So although we do have a considerable number of written prayers from this period, they are for the most part described as models for those whose ability to pray *ex tempore* was restricted. And from this we must further presume that within limits local uses and local conventions were fully accepted.

It might be tempting for us to assign deep historical and theological significance to the practice of *ex tempore* eucharistic praying in this period on the assumption that the early church's pastoral liturgists had deliberately chosen it as a unique approach to public prayer. But certainly the relationship between written and *ex tempore* forms of liturgical prayer had exact parallels with modes of public discourse in other disciplines in this period, especially in education, politics, and law.[14] The formal skills of classical rhetoric were assumed to provide a basis for well-developed oral expression in most professions, but for those individuals who felt the need, a written outline or pattern was provided, along with a summary of the stylistic conventions. In an age when the duplication of individual texts was a highly labor-intensive occupation, local uses and local conventions dominated in all professions.

The shift from primarily extemporized liturgical prayer offered "within the conventions" to a primarily text-based liturgy, in which not only the conventions, but also the exact words were clearly specified, was a slow one, but seems largely to have been complete in the West by about the mid-sixth century.[15] An indication of the direction things are headed is found in a decree of the Council of Milevis (401 C.E.):[16]

> It was decided that prayers or orations or masses that had been approved in council should be used by all—whether prefaces, commendations, or hand-layings—and that others contrary to the faith should not be proffered at all, but only those collected by the more judicious should be said.[17]

In his survey of the development of eucharistic praying in this period, Allan Bouley outlines the motivations and processes by which written liturgical texts became the norm for liturgical praying. He attributes the change to:

1. the fourth-century and fifth-century doctrinal controversies that demanded a liturgy that could be shown to be "orthodox."[18]
2. the missionary expansion of the church within a situation of political instability.
3. the increasing complexity of the calendar and expansion of the number of feast days and saint's days, which required a variable set of prayers.
4. the increasing complexity of the "models" as literary efforts in their own right, and hence the increasing difficulty in following them. Often the names of respected authors became attached to these texts (correctly or incorrectly), and this gained for them a certain inviolability.[19]

While all of these things, and especially doctrinal and political instability, are certainly essential motivating factors in the trend toward a fully scripted liturgy, changes in the way information was processed and transmitted must also be taken into account. And because of this, I would want to add to Bouley's list the impact of the system of monastic and public scriptoria, which became increasingly well-organized between the fifth and seventh centuries, for the production of multiple copies of a given text.[20] But for a number of reasons that shall become evident, even this new "information-processing technology" did not produce the kind of uniformity that is usually associated with early-medieval liturgical practice.

The attempt to reconstruct the history of the early-medieval scribal system is fraught with difficulties. Not only is there a lack of solid information, but what information there is points to the fact that scribal culture existed in sufficiently diverse shapes and forms to make confident generalization almost impossible. The scribes working at the Great Library at Alexandria in the fifth century operated under different conditions from those in the book shops of eleventh-century Paris, or from those in the Abbey of St. Albans, or from those in a public scriptorium in Rome. But some things can be said about this information-processing system, and particularly about its limitations.

In the ordinary scriptorium, whether monastic or public, one person dictated the manuscript to be duplicated to a gathering of scribes, who attempted to copy it word-for-word as it was read.[21] On occasion for a special copy of a particular book (and liturgical books often fell into this category), one scribe would work independently from one original. With this in mind, the question arises: What was being attempted and what was actually achieved by this process? And our immediate response to both questions is likely to be: "The mass production of exact duplicates of a manuscript original." But part of the difficulty with this answer is that it is heavily laden with the values of our own print-oriented culture. Historian Elizabeth Eisenstein warns that "uniformity and synchronization have become so common since the advent of printing that we have to remind ourselves repeatedly that they were usually absent in the age of the scribes."[22] In no real sense, she adds, can we talk of "duplication" in this period, or of an "edition" of a particular text.[23] Both are "post-print" ideas.

This is especially true for liturgical manuscripts since two particular elements in the scribal system were working against the "duplication" liturgical texts. First, there was an increased margin of error if the text in question was being copied by a single scribe working from a single manuscript original (the quality and accuracy of which was itself uncertain). Second, the likelihood of faithful reproduction of a liturgical manuscript was substantially reduced if it was being copied by a monk under discipline of the Rule and the *opus dei* in a monastic community. Indeed, the monastic scriptoria must have been the very worst places to get an exact duplicate of a liturgical book.

The monk was a crucial component of medieval information-processing technology, and his relationship with the liturgy shaped the possibilities of that technology in a significant way. Day after day and year after year, the liturgy exerted a powerful influence on the life of a monk. It was internalized by every member of the community and stood in a relationship of authority over every activity, including the act of copying. Thus, if the details of a liturgical manuscript as it was being copied differed significantly from the liturgy as it was being experienced, then it was quite likely that the manuscript would be altered to put it into alignment with the monk's own liturgical experience.[24]

And so despite the increased *desire* on the part of church authorities for a fixed and invariable set of liturgical texts from the sixth century onward, the information-processing technology available could not substantially accommodate that desire. There was, of course, throughout this period, a growing consensus about the content of liturgical prayer, matched by sanctions against those who deviated from that consensus. But local and regional variations persisted, not only because of their own natural vigor, but also because of the character of the scribal system by which texts were produced. At no time before the advent of print in the mid-fifteenth century, therefore, can we say with any confidence that written liturgies are "fixed and invariable."

This discrepancy between the desire for uniformity and the ability to achieve it began to put real pressure on the scriptoria, and especially the monastic scriptoria. But there were also economic pressures. A large book such as a Bible or antiphonary took the hides of between two hundred and three hundred sheep or calves, and the preparation of these hides was a time-consuming and difficult task. However, in about the mid-thirteenth century, as a by-product of the growing European textile industry, cheap and plentiful linen rag paper began to be produced.[25] This meant that increasingly labor was the most expensive part of the bookmaking enterprise. The scriptoria were simply a too labor-intensive method of producing books to survive.

THE PRINTING PRESS

The invention of printing with moveable type brought about the most radical transformation in the conditions of intellectual life in the history of Western Civilization. . . . Its effects were sooner or later felt in every department of human activity.[26]

Such hyperbole is common when historians discuss the printing press. But something of a sense that a revolution had happened must have also been felt at the time. Johannes Gutenberg set up his press in Mainz in 1450, and within thirty-five years every major state had an important publishing center. By 1490, for example, there were over one thousand public presses in Germany alone (not to mention those in monasteries or private houses)—each one producing large quantities of sermon collections, indulgences,[27] religious tracts, and catechisms.[28] Print technology, rising literacy, religion, and economics together were forging a powerful coalition.[29]

But even with the rapid popularity of the printing press, the age of the scribes did not abruptly end. Monks were advised to keep on copying by hand because it was useful for occupying idle hands, learning Scripture, and developing habits of diligence and devotion.[30] It also seems that a large number of books in the late-fifteenth century were being copied by scribes from printed originals.[31] Conversely, the religious orders often consigned work to local presses (some monasteries also had presses of their own), and in the early stages printers retained scribal conventions in their work.

The printing press is so connected in the historical imagination with the Continental Reformation that it is sometimes surprising to realize how well established it had already become in Martin Luther's day. The first German Bible was printed in 1466, seventeen years before Luther was born. During this period, peripatetic Bible sellers peddled their wares from town to town,[32] and vernacular printed Bibles were plentiful, not only in German but also in French, Saxon, Dutch, Italian, Spanish, and Bohemian.[33] Polyglot versions were also extremely popular. The debt the Continental Reformation owes to the spread of biblical literacy already established at the beginning of the sixteenth century and fostered by the printing press is only recently beginning to be appreciated.[34]

In his *Actes and Monuments,* John Foxe (1624–91) writes confidently:

> How many presses there be in the world, so many block houses there be against the high castle of St Angelo, so that either the pope must abolish knowledge and printing, or printing must at length root him out.[35]

And even though for the first sixty-five years of its existence, the printing press produced materials that supported the official doctrine, liturgy, and piety of the church,[36] Foxe's central insight was correct. The same forces that fostered the press were also at work in fostering the Reformation: the rise of the merchant class, increased literacy, enthusiastic lay piety, and the expansion of trade. Printing "eliminated the class monopoly on knowledge" and "democratized the making of images."[37] And it broke the clerical monopoly as well, the clerical monopoly on liturgical knowledge and on the making of liturgical images.[38] So while on the one hand liturgists like Luther, Calvin, and Cranmer relied upon the fact that "changes that might have taken centuries to achieve through the circulation of manuscripts took place almost overnight through the agency of print,"[39] on the other hand, they also must have known that the literate person-in-the-pew with a service book in hand would have to have a far greater say in the kind of liturgy that they were offered.[40] (The Devonshire and Norfolk rebellions which followed the imposition of Cranmer's first *Book of Common Prayer* in 1549 are eloquent testimony to the degree to which this democratization of worship was operative.)

And so with the adoption of the printing press the total liturgical uniformity so earnestly desired by the Catholic Church for over nine hundred years was technologically achievable; but ironically, at the very moment that it became achievable, it also became impossible.

The press was an indispensable agent in the fracture of the church's liturgical tradition. In the early years of the Reformation, print technology made possible both the dissemination of increasingly diverse and distinctive worship traditions, and in the centuries that followed it allowed for the consolidation of those traditions into the various worship "families."[41]

But print technology also made possible the strong conservative reaction to the Reformation, which was liturgically embodied in the rites promulgated after the Council of Trent (1545–63). Indeed, one commentator has described Trent as a "rear-guard action designed to contain the forces that Gutenberg's invention had unleashed."[42] For the next four hundred years, the Tridentine rites remained virtually unaltered and were imposed almost universally, and the task of the Roman Catholic liturgist became almost entirely interpretive rather than creative.

THE COMPUTER REVOLUTION

The most recent decisive change in information processing has come with the advent of the modern computer, and particularly with the advances in microprocessing, which made personal computers and word processors possible. Developments in this area have been so rapid that what most people in the West now take for granted (the possibility of a computer in every home, for example) was considered science fiction just thirty years ago, but now artificial intelligence (AI) is a major area of academic and philosophical inquiry.[43] For most of its history, the computer has been closely linked to printing, although with the growth of networking systems and electronic mail that link is now rapidly dissolving.[44]

For those responsible for the churches' liturgy, the changes occasioned by the use of computers have been both subtle and profound. A few years ago, the North American Academy of Liturgy began briefing sessions for computer users at its annual meetings, and since then the number in attendance at these sessions has mushroomed. The range of resources that have been digitized for the use of liturgists is growing rapidly: bibliographies, periodical indexes, editions of ancient texts, and congregational music and worship aids are all available on-line. One recently introduced interactive information base describes itself as having been designed to "provide electronic access to iconographic, architectural and geographic resources, primary texts and translation, dictionaries, slides, music and video" to users:[45]

> For example, if a slide of Ste. Chapelle is brought up on the computer screen, paths to other resources related to it are accessible—texts on historical background, slides which review architectural style, slides of similar chapels, music samples which may have been heard in the chapel at the time it was constructed.[46]

In addition to tapping into this sort of information resource, people at various levels of liturgical responsibility are using computers in various other ways. At the denominational and interdenominational level, computer networks can enable teams of people in various parts of the nation (or the world) to work together on a common liturgical task. Most often, in practice, this task has been the development and revision of liturgical texts, and increasingly, the participants in the computer network also have access to various liturgical databases. At the local level, pastors and others are designing congregational liturgy on the computer screen and producing texts and compilations of texts with the aid of desktop publishing systems. The use of computer technology in these ways has several implications for the outcome of the process, but of these, three in particular are worth mentioning.

1. It increases the number of sources of liturgical input.

The ease of access to databases and to the opinions of colleagues all over the world encourages historical and theological cross-fertilization on a scale unknown to liturgists of the past.[47] But this can have both positive and negative results. On the positive side, the worship of a denomination or congregation can be deepened and enriched by a creative recovery of the liturgical treasures of the past and a creative application of the best liturgical thinking of the present. But on the other hand, there can be serious difficulties when the contents of a given liturgical rite or text is culled from a wide variety of liturgical sources (which may represent a wide variety of theological perspectives). A composite rite of this sort may embody internal contradictions, or it may contradict the worship tradition and theology of the group that is to use it.

2. It encourages quantities of liturgical "ephemera."

At the local level especially, the ease with which worship materials can be produced and published can lead to liturgy being experienced as a disposable commodity. The sense that a given act of worship is a self-contained experience, unrelated in form or content to the acts of worship that precede and follow it, is familiar to many congregations since the advent of the personal computer. This raises, of course, the larger question of whether or not there can be a "one-time" liturgy, or whether liturgy by its very nature as ritual must be regularly and invariably repeated and thus thoroughly internalized by its participants. But many of those involved in the computerization of liturgy would say that what is more important is the fidelity to a core of tradition, to a set of euchological conventions upon which to build a modern liturgical prayer life.[48]

3. It obscures the antecedents of a particular rite.

While computers make possible the rapid production of both *ad hoc* worship services on the local level and official texts on the denominational or national level, they also tend to obscure the historical and theological roots of the resulting material. At the simplest level, revising a particular text by computer often means eliminating previous drafts; the author simply writes over the unwanted material and deletes it. As a result, following the line of thought that led to a rite or text is increasingly difficult.[49] The wider concern is that this will increase the historical and theological parochialism of contemporary worship, that the computer allows local concerns to supersede traditional liturgical structures.

Clearly, professional liturgical work has been deeply affected by the coming of computers and desktop publishing systems. And many would say that the changes we have highlighted above are all unambiguously destructive of the common prayer of the Christian people. But perhaps we have simply returned to a situation very similar to that which prevailed in the early church. Local uses, improvised liturgical prayer, the sense that what is truly important is to pray "within the conventions," and that the ability to pray "to the best of one's ability" have returned as doxological standards. If so, the circle that carried Christian liturgical praying from freedom to formula to uniformity has now begun to carry it back to its origins.

THE BUREAUCRATIZATION OF THE LITURGY

In the classic book on the psycho-social impact of technology *The Homeless Mind* the authors describe the hallmarks of technologized modernity. One of the principal elements in the technological "cluster of consciousness" is a pervasive and progressive tendency toward bureaucratization. Bureaucracy is the principal mechanism by which the values and processes of a technological society are transmitted to the individual, and by which the balance of the technological system is managed and maintained. The "homeless mind" presupposes that "everything is organizable" and that bureaucratic forms can be applied "in principle to just about any human phenomenon":[50]

> Bureaucracy is not only orderly, but orderly in an imperialistic mode. There is a bureaucratic demiurge who views the universe as dumb chaos waiting to be brought into the redeeming order of bureaucratic administration.[51]

As the wide use of the term *institutional church* testifies, this "bureaucratic demiurge" has translated itself into large-scale organizational structures that regulate the life of almost every denomination throughout the world.[52] Sociologist of religion Robert Wuthnow describes the progress of bureaucracy within the American churches:

> To the huge denominational bureaucracies that were erected earlier in the century have now been added dozens of highly institutionalized organizations oriented to special interest groups within denominations, to coordinating the complex relations among denominations, and to filling in the crevices with religious activities that denominations have not provided.[53]

Among the most heavily bureaucratized areas of the churches' life has been Christian worship. While it is true that since the establishment of the Congregation of Sacred Rites in 1588 there have always been groups which saw themselves as having general oversight in the production and implementation of service materials, the expansion and diversification of liturgical boards and agencies, commissions, congregations, and organized pressure groups in the past fifty years has mirrored the bureaucratic tendencies in society at large.[54] Today in the Standing Liturgical Commission of the Episcopal Church (USA), the Section on Worship of the Board of Discipleship of The United Methodist Church, the Worship Office of the Presbyterian Church (USA), the Inter-Lutheran Commission on Worship,[55] and in many other such bodies, those concerned with the public prayer of their respective denominations work in a specifically bureaucratic context. In addition, this trend toward bureaucratization has spilled over into the liturgical lives not only of denominations but also (by a sort of ecclesiastical "trickle-down" process) of congregations and individual worshipers as well.

Although there are other components of the technological "cluster of consciousness" besides the bureaucratic, and other analyses of technologized modernity that do not lay such heavy emphasis on bureaucratic processes,[56] certainly the pervasiveness of bureaucratic liturgizing demands that we take a careful look at the specific ways in which it may shape the experience of worship for individuals and groups. A close inspection of the various characteristics of the bureaucratic system, and serious attention to the several messages that it sends, raises a number of questions for late-twentieth-century liturgists and worshipers: Can worship that is bureaucratically conditioned serve the spiritual and liturgical needs of diverse congregations and individuals? Is this the way we *intend* to arrange our liturgical lives as Christian believers? And (perhaps more to the point), is this the way we *want* to arrange our liturgical lives?

The first characteristic of bureaucracy relates to the system and its output. Bureaucratic systems tend toward the establishment of arenas of competence, toward the compartmentalization of that competence, a reliance on proper procedure, orderliness, and predictability. Every bureaucracy must produce a system of categories within which everything can be handled.[57] Because of this, institutional bureaucracy in general is a system that, while it may not in every case intentionally suppress creativity, at the very least it aims at a form of carefully managed creativity.[58]

In most cases liturgical commissions, boards, or agencies receive their support and their mandate for work from the governing body of the denomination in question, often through one or more intermediate institutional structures. The Section on Worship of The United Methodist Church, for example, working as a subunit of the Board of Discipleship, is ultimately responsible to General Conference, which both authorizes its work initially and approves it at various stages of development. And similar control over liturgical work is exercised by general synods, general conventions, and general assemblies in the various Christian denominations.

When the denominational governing body authorizes a piece of liturgical work, whether it be a minor revision to the funeral service or an entirely new hymnal, the project enters the bureaucratic system and is, in large measure, immediately conformed to it. Liturgy has become a problem to be solved, and the institutional structures are quickly marshaled to attack the job at hand. Subcommittees, task forces, and procedural flowcharts begin to break the work down into its component parts, and to delimit the number of different kinds of interaction possible on the project as a whole. Particular needs are identified and categorized, and consultants are drawn in to bring expertise to specific aspects of the project. This kind of compartmentalization of work effectively narrows the range of sources of creative input and limits the cross-fertilization of ideas that foster liturgical creativity. Very often a project will be seen to be "complete" at the moment when the various individual components can be assembled into a single package.[59] The effects of this kind of compartmentalization can be seen in a response to *Baptism, Eucharist, and Ministry* from the Church in Wales:

> The Church in Wales in authorizing new liturgical services did not involve the Doctrine Commission or ask it to produce a theological statement on them. It entrusted full responsibility to the Liturgical Commission to produce baptismal and eucharistic services. Since the prime function of that body is to produce draft services, it was hardly able to examine as fully as the Doctrine Commission some of the theological and doctrinal principles un-

derlying those services. Is that the right way to proceed? The effect is that since *lex orandi* is *lex credendi* the Liturgical Commission has charge of doctrine as well as liturgy.[60]

There are occasions when the members (or the paid professional staff) of a liturgical commission may engage with others in creative "brainstorming" sessions in order to respond to a particular liturgical need. Often these sessions do result in proposals that fall outside the predefined scope of their work, or move across predefined areas of interest and expertise. But in most cases the proposals cannot be acted upon until they are processed through the system,[61] and since this can take a number of months or years, the spontaneity and the creative energy is often depleted. At other times the system so thoroughly reshapes the proposal that it is unrecognizable.

Equally, a creative idea from *outside* the system can suffer at the hands of the liturgical bureaucracy. Often these ideas do not fall neatly within the predetermined categories of the system, or overlap two or more different categories.[62] Since it is easier for the system to reject such an idea than to manufacture for itself a new category to deal with it, many ideas from outside the system are lost to the church in the bureaucratic process. Creativity is similarly lost in the assessment of liturgical need, since again, predetermined categories often define the areas in which such need is expected to fall.

Because any bureaucratic system tends to suppress creative energy in these ways, to the extent that a denomination or congregation values worship that is open to the spirit of creativity it will be less than satisfied with liturgies that have been strained through bureaucratic structures. But it can certainly be argued that in the area of Christian worship, creativity is not necessarily something to be encouraged. Tradition, stability, conserving the treasures of the past, and handing them on intact to future generations—this is the function of the church where its worship is concerned. Perhaps, then, bureaucracy can serve the cause of liturgical conservatism?

But ironically, bureaucratic liturgical structures are just as effective at discouraging the preservation of tradition as they are at discouraging creativity. This is because they are specifically established for and devoted to managing *change*. They feed on problems to be solved, goals to be attained, and deadlines to be met. They define objectives (or have objectives defined for them by others) and to the extent that an emphasis on maintaining and recapitulating a particular worship tradition constrains the achievement of these defined objectives, it must be seen as something of a problem for the liturgical bureaucrat.

Hence we can see why the Pentecostalist traditions on the one hand, with their radical sense of openness to the creativity of the Holy Spirit in worship, and the Greek and Russian Orthodox traditions on the other hand, with their radical sense of the fixity of the ancient liturgical tradition, have no desire or need for a worship bureaucracy. At the two ends of the liturgical spectrum, bureaucracy is useless. But in the liturgical center, among those who aim for some sort of balance between the liturgical demands of tradition and the liturgical needs of the present and future in their worship, bureaucratic structures have flourished.[63]

Overall, however, bureaucratically produced liturgy carries with it a sense of discontinuity with the past, rather than a sense that it is the product of a natural evolution from previous forms of worship. This sense of discontinuity is heightened by the system of copyrighting the output of the bureaucracy.[64] The copyright on a liturgical text has the same function as a patent on an invention: it protects the author or inventor from those who would claim the work as their own and ensures that any profits from the work return to its creator.[65] But a significant by-product of this process is the sense of the historical isolation of the copyrighted material. As historian of technology George Basalla says:

> In the process [of patenting], an invention is uniquely identified with its inventor and its associations with existing artifacts are obscured. . . . A patent bestows societal recognition on an inventor and distorts the extent of the debt owed to the past by encouraging concealment of the network of ties that lead from earlier related artifacts.[66]

In other words, as soon as a work is clearly identified with a particular author, institution, or group it loses some of its claim to be in continuity with the tradition. The holder of a patent or copyright asserts that there is enough new and different in the work to separate it both from the work of others who might claim authorship and also from the natural outworking of historical processes. So the copyrighted product of a liturgical bureaucracy not only "feels" somewhat alien because of the process by which it is produced, by virtue of bearing a copyright it is officially *declared* to be somewhat alien by those who promulgate it.

This relationship between the attachment of specific texts to specific authors and the detachment of those texts from historical processes can be seen clearly in the preface to a recent book of worship resources produced for use by the Christian Church (Disciples of Christ). In a section entitled "A Note About Copyright," the compilers of *Thankful Praise* say:[67]

> Most materials in this book have been developed by the writers as new compositions or as extensively edited resources, in most cases not previously published. Many of the compositions and other resources use phrases or ideas drawn from Scripture, usually the Revised Standard Version. Even when resources follow the scripture text quite closely, the passages have usually been adapted freely for liturgical use.[68]

Besides disrupting the relationship between contemporary liturgy and its historical antecedents, the copyright system may also disrupt the relationship between contemporary liturgy and theology. In his 1984 book *On Liturgical Theology*, Aidan Kavanagh explores some of the reasons why the liturgy no longer functions as "primary theology," a vital source and foundation of the community's thinking about God, "the dynamic condition under which theological reflection is done."[69] He claims that in the past the creative relationship between Christian corporate worship and theology was heavily dependent on the "anonymity" of the liturgy:

> The human agents of first order enterprises such as liturgy and language are usually anonymous. We do not know who spoke the first word or sang the first poem any more than we know . . . who presided at the first eucharist after the Last Supper, or when; . . . or who composed almost any ancient liturgical text or originated almost any ceremonial gesture one might care to name. The point is that in first order matters anonymity is the rule, intentions are obscure, and meaning is less precise than it is richly ambiguous.[70]

In other words, part of the difficulty with the copyrighting of liturgical material is that it contributes to a larger "nailing-down" process that effectively reduces the possibilities of interpretation of the liturgical event. To identify the liturgy as having been generated by a specific person or group forces the community to enter the experience of worship through a relatively narrow gate. The creative ambiguity of liturgical symbolism, the open-ended riskiness of liturgical poetry, the holy playfulness of liturgical prayer and ceremony is at least partially subverted by the static precision of a copyrighted, bureaucratically produced liturgical text.

If the liturgical *product* is profoundly influenced by the denominational bureaucracy, so too is the liturgical "clientele," the individual congregation or worshiper. In any bureaucracy there is a strong impetus toward the anonymity of the client, since the system aims at "reducing the concrete individual to a 'case,' a 'number,' or a member of a certain class, respectively, without significant remainder."[71] People fall into abstract categories, and although the system is often disturbed by "eruptions of concrete humanity,"[72] on the whole the successful working of the operation depends on identifying and meeting the needs of the "typical" client. Because of this, individual needs tend to be suppressed and depersonalization takes over. (It is this feature of the system that caused Jean-Paul Sartre to speak of the human spirit as a "victim" of bureaucracy.)[73]

The system achieves the radical depersonalization of the individual client in a number of ways. First, it imposes control on the spontaneous expression of emotion, and indeed, one of the functions of a bureaucracy is to *assign* emotional states to its clients.[74] In other words, the feedback from client to bureaucracy is carefully managed (by, for example, the use of jargon or statistical survey methods), and this necessarily leads to a relatively passive involvement on the part of the client. "In short, bureaucracy transforms subjects (individuals as self-creative projects) into objects."[75]

Given this description, is it understandable that many individuals and congregations feel alienated from the system that governs the overall shape of their liturgical life, as well as from the various products of that system (including official hymnals, liturgical texts, worship guidelines, and the policies governing the liturgical training of ministers and other worship leaders). In the process of bureaucratization, says Franz Neumann, "Human relations lose their directness and become mediated by third parties, public or private functionaries seated more or less securely in power, authoritatively prescribe the behavior of man."[76]

The alienation that is a by-product of this process causes not only deep pastoral-liturgical difficulties, but theological difficulties as well with the status and authority of bureaucratically imposed liturgies.

From ancient times, the principle of "reception" has governed the degree to which an official ecclesiastical document of any kind could claim authority.[77] Although the term has historically been applied to the pronouncements of church councils, more recently reception has been of vital significance in discussions of the validity of contemporary ecumenical instruments and liturgical rites.[78] True reception always involves more than simply a passive acceptance, or even a general endorsement, of an official act by local communities of faith. Rather "reception is a profound appropriation, through a gradual testing, by which teachings are made part of the life and liturgy of the community."[79] (For example, the growing fixity of the canon of Scripture can be seen to be the result of a process of reception, in which the Gospels and later the Epistles and other biblical material eventually came to be accepted as expressive of the very heart of the Christian experience.)[80] In every case, reception serves both to integrate the various levels of ecclesiastical authority and to affirm the *sensus fidelium*.

Liturgical reception is rooted in the conviction that the worship experience of each community of faith is of real value as a source of theological and doctrinal reflection. But clearly, contemporary forms of liturgical bureaucracy raise questions for the theological and practical status of reception because of the degree to which the bureaucracy disenfranchises the individual worshiper or congregation as a dialogue partner in the process of liturgical revision. In many cases the worshiping community has become simply a passive receptacle into which liturgy (and also theology) is poured from above, and the authority of its own liturgical experience is discounted. Aidan Kavanagh describes the situation:

> The liturgical assembly, which has been meeting under God fifty-two times a year for the past 2,000 years, now must be regarded as a theological cipher drawing whatever theological awareness it has not from its own graced encounter with the living God, but from sources found in ecclesiastical bureaucracies and within the

walls of academe. The served has become servant, the mistress has become handmaid.[81]

CONCLUSION

This chapter has focused on two aspects of the relationship between Christian worship and technology. The first involved the interaction between changing technology and liturgical work and the second involved the ways in which technology's "management and distribution system," the bureaucracy, shapes both the liturgical product and the liturgical clientele. In passing we have raised a number of questions that contemporary liturgists and contemporary worshipers need to face: Can the creative possibilities of the computer be reconciled with the need for reference to a historical and theological tradition? Does a highly compartmentalized system encourage sufficient cross-fertilization between, for example, liturgy and doctrine, liturgy and social justice, liturgy and religious education? Does the restriction of feedback and the anonymity that the bureaucracy imposes on the clientele actively discourage community and individual "ownership" of parochial liturgy? Can intentionally arbitrary systems take account of the wide variety of needs and desires that liturgical praxis is designed to meet? Is modern information technology making for us a new "patristic age" of liturgical praying? Can a system in which highly educated experts attempt to meet the needs of the stereotypical clients ensure respect for cultural, racial, and socioeconomic diversity? In short, are bureaucratic liturgical structures and sophisticated information-processing systems good for the public prayer of the Christian people?

Ironically, the two kinds of technological influences we have been discussing, information processing and bureaucratization, may be pulling the "shape" of contemporary liturgical work in two opposite directions. On the one hand, ever since the advent of print information, technology has increasingly given power to those at the grass roots, and this is particularly true with the most recent developments in microcomputers.[82] At the same time, the centralizing and hierarchic tendencies of bureaucracy have also increased dramatically. Whether these two forces will balance each other (or cancel out the other's effects), or whether one force or another will gain command over the processes by which worship is shaped, has yet to be determined.

CHAPTER
FOUR

WORSHIP AND TECHNOLOGY IN HISTORY, 1: MEDIEVAL ENGINEERING AND THE LITURGY

Unbelieving philosophers . . . Arabs, Hebrews and Greeks, who dwell among Christians, as in Spain, Egypt, parts of the East, and in many other regions of the world, abhor the folly which they behold in the arrangement of the chronology followed by the Christians in their festivals.[1]

This is the lament of Franciscan friar Roger Bacon (1214?–92), by all accounts the greatest experimental scientist of the Middle Ages: that the liturgical calendar was in such a state of disarray that it was a serious barrier to the spread of Christianity. How it got to be that way, and how Bacon and others applied the most advanced technical and mathematical tools of the day to the problem of calendar reform, is a significant episode in the story of the interplay between engineering technology and liturgy.

Between the early-twelfth and mid-fourteenth[2] centuries there existed in the Latin West a cooperative relationship between Christian faith and scientific technology which has never been equaled. Great scientist-theologians such as Peter Abelard, Robert Grosseteste, Bernard of Chartres, Richard of Wallingford, and Bacon,[3] having reaped a rich harvest of ideas and insights with the recent translations of Greek and Arabic scientific treatises,[4] applied experimental reason to a variety of both theological and practical problems. One of the hallmarks of this period was the development of increasingly accurate systems of measurement.[5] In such fields as navigation, timekeeping, and manufacturing there were explosions of progress as a result of the invention of new and more precise instrumentation. This is the age of the magnetic compass, the mechanical clock, practical geometry, optics (and, as a result, eyeglasses),[6] and of the advances in architectural engineering which found their expression in the great cathedrals.

This same passion for exactitude carried over into the areas of astrology and astronomy, both of which "fascinated the best minds of the time because [they] provided a total vision of reality, uniting the macrocosm to the human microcosm."[7] The practical applications of more precise astrological and astronomical computations were many, and medicine and commerce especially benefited.[8] But it was the reform of the calendar that would permanently bind the history of Christian worship to the history of this aspect of technological and scientific innovation.

A calendar has been virtually essential to every religion in history. Indeed, it is often suggested that the liturgical needs of ancient religion (in conjunction with the rise of planned agricultural communities) was the principal force behind the development of the calendar itself.[9] In Bacon's time, the calendar in use was that developed by Julius Caesar in 46 B.C.E., and in the 1200 years since its imposition computational errors had put it approximately 10 days out of alignment with the seasons.[10] The principal difficulty arising from this discrepancy in the Julian calendar was the accurate computation of the date of Easter, but the determination of other dates in the Christian calendar that depended on the date of Easter (the so-called movable feasts) was also of real concern. Because these dates were based on both the lunar and the solar calendars, the principles of calculation, called *computus*, were quite complex, and the question gave rise to multiple solutions. The best minds of the age were turned to this matter, and no fewer than eighty learned treatises on the subject were written between 526 and 1003 by theologians of the stature of Alcuin, Isidore of Seville, Walafrid Strabo, and Bede.[11] Much of this work was undertaken within the walls of monasteries.

But interest in *computus* was more than just simply for the sake of ecclesiastical accuracy, or even, as Bacon had argued, for the sake of the mission of the church. It was a matter vital to salvation itself:

> Life and prayer were corporate and followed the majestic cycle of the Christian year. The personal fulfillment of a monk came in his sharing in the solemn ecstasy of the orderly succession of liturgies and the choreography of the seasons. The greatest of these was Easter, yet also the crucial variable dominating everything from Septuagesima Sunday until Trinity, a period of nearly four months. Computus told a monk how, by calculating solar and lunar motions, he could rightly worship and thus achieve his destiny.[12]

And more widely still, the monastic life was, in a very real sense, caught up in the great "drama enacted between Heaven and Hell" in which the cycle of the Christian year was a vital weapon.[13] Thus, to the degree that the liturgical calendar was accurate, some anxiety about the salvation of both the individual and the world as a whole could be relieved.[14]

Roger Bacon had identified several errors in the calendar, and outlined them in his important treatise, the *Opus Majus* (1267). In addition to the simple contradiction between the observable celestial motions and the calendar dating itself,[15] there was the more specific matter of the date of Easter and the Lenten fast which immediately preceded it. As the error accumulated, "Not only Easter but Lent and all the moveable feasts will recede in a shocking fashion from their positions and the whole order of the ecclesiastical office will be confused. . . . In the real Lent, meats will be eaten for many days."[16]

The computations on which Bacon based his critique of the calendar were worked out with the aid of a number of scientific instruments, of which the *astrolabe*, a kind of sextant for calculating the positions of the stars and planets, was the most usual and in fairly wide use by astronomers of the period.[17] (The fact that Peter Abelard named his son "Astrolabe" is both an indication of the status of this instrument in intellectual circles and a testimony to faith in the future of science.) "Skillful astronomers have no doubt that all these statements are facts," Bacon asserted. "Moreover, every computer knows that the beginning of the moon's cycle is in error by three to four days."[18] Bacon made a number of recommendations designed both to rectify the immediate situation as well as to ensure that the calendar remained in alignment in the future. But here we begin to see that the reaction of church authorities to proposals with a technological component is sometimes less than positive.

Bacon presented his ideas to Pope Clement IV (1265–68), but his earnest appeal to reform the scandalous errors of the Julian calendar went unheeded.[19] Moreover, his other theories about such things as the possibility of finding a sea route to India ("The water . . . extends for no great width between the end of Spain and the beginning of India.")[20] and his reliance on "pagan authorities" such as Averroes combined with his attack on corruption in the church, led to his official condemnation in 1277.[21] But Bacon's efforts would not be utterly wasted; they would provide a firm foundation for work on the technology needed to reform the liturgical calendar which continued into the next two centuries. This time, however, more advanced computations were based upon the mechanical successor to the astrolabe.

In about 1330 Richard of Wallingford, the eccentric abbot of the Benedictine monastery of St. Albans, devised two influential astronomical instruments, which he called the *albion* and the *rectangulus.* The albion was a mechanical scale designed to determine accurately the positions of the planets, and the rectangulus was a sort of miniature planetarium, which demonstrated the relative positions of the sun, the moon, the planets, and the stars. Over two hundred years later, this *geometricum instrumentum* could be seen in the Abbey church, as one visitor from 1540 tells us: "One may look at the course of the sun and moon or the fixed stars or again one may regard the rise and fall of the tides."[22] From the calculations made using this machine, Richard wrote an illustrated book that exerted considerable influence on astronomers and navigators. But still the ecclesiastical authorities resisted the reformation of the liturgical calendar.

Less than 100 years later, Cardinal Pierre d'Ailly (1350–1420), himself the author of several scientific works, was appointed to make a recommendation on the matter of calendar reform to the Council of Constance (1414–18).[23] Citing the work of Bacon and Abbot Richard, d'Ailly declared the Julian calendar to be nine days out of alignment and urged immediate action. But even then, nothing was done.

It was not until 1582, nearly three centuries after Bacon demonstrated the serious flaws in a Christian year ordered according to the Julian calendar, that a reform was ordered by Gregory XIII (1572–85). In that year Gregory removed ten days from the calendar (October 5, 1582 became October 15, 1582) and, following Bacon's three-hundred-year-old advice, declared that only the centurial years that were divisible by four hundred would be leap years in order to ensure that the calendar would remain true to the celestial observations.[24] In the end, the technology of the astrolabe, the albion, and the rectangulus had finally turned the course of liturgical history, and the computational advances they made possible continue to this day to set the date of Easter.

Residual problems with the calendar continue to attract the interest of theologians and astronomers, encouraged by those who desire a more stable and symmetrical scheme. In 1923, the League of Nations set up a "Calendar Commission" (which received over two hundred separate proposals for calendar reform in the fourteen years of its existence), and a World Calendar Association was founded in New York in 1930.[25] Astronomers, using increasingly precise instruments, continue to provide solutions to calendrical problems, and a recent plan by a Belgian astronomer offers a calendar that will take 30,000 years to be one day out of alignment with the solar calendar.

The call for a fixed date for Easter is heard frequently among the Christian churches in the late-twentieth century, and especially as they come to terms with the growing pluralism and secularism of society at large. In its 1975 Assembly in Nairobi, the World Council of Churches made a serious attempt to fix the date of Easter, but all solutions were blocked by resistance to change on the part of the Orthodox and Eastern Rite churches. Adolf Adam, as a part of his explication of the historical roots of the liturgical calendar, offered his opinion of the current situation:

The growing assimilation of peoples and continents and their modern economies calls for a fixed and easily grasped chronological order with a uniform rhythm of workdays and holidays, times of work and times of leisure. For statistics on work, productivity schedules, and long-range planning the irregular occurrence of Christian holy days raises difficulties that merit serious consideration.[26]

Adam's view seems to be representative of a fairly wide body of opinion which today cuts across the national and denominational spectrum. If this is so, it is clear that the influence of technology on the shape of the Christian calendar did not come to an end in the sixteenth century. Although astronomy will have a part to play in increasing the precision of the calendar, it will be the more insistent demands of industrial technology—"statistics on work, productivity schedules and long-range planning"—which will be the most potent force in shaping the future of the liturgical calendar.

CLOCK TIME AND THE LITURGICAL LIFE

The impact of machines such as Richard of Wallingford's *geometricum instrumentum* on Christian worship would not end with the revision of the liturgical calendar. A direct descendant of the *horologium*[27] was to be the force behind an even more massive change, not only in liturgy, but in all of human life. The mechanical clock

> synchronized human actions, not with the rising and setting sun, but with the indicated movements of the clock's hands: so it brought exact measurement and temporal control into every activity, by setting an independent standard whereby the whole day could be laid out and subdivided.[28]

The story of the development of the mechanical clock is a fascinating one, and is interwoven with the story of the monastic and parochial liturgy from the sixth century onward.[29] Time measurement was of particular importance in the monastery, and especially for those who followed the Rule attributed to St. Benedict of Nursia (c. 480–c. 550), who is called the "Father of Western Monasticism." *Laborare et orare*, to work and to pray: this was the calling of the Benedictine monk. But while work was important ("Idleness is the enemy of the soul," Benedict had warned), at the heart of the monastic life, and that from which all other activities took their inspiration, was the *opus dei*, the recitation of the daily office.[30] That this should always be performed at the correct time was crucial: "To give the signal for the *opus dei,* whether by day or by night, is the responsibility of the Abbot. He may do it himself or he may lay the charge on a brother sufficiently responsible to ensure that everything is performed at the correct time."[31]

Any talk about the "reformation" of a monastery, usually meant the reestablishment of the proper times and sequences of the Divine Office, and the ensuring that *"omnia horis competentibus compleantur*—all things be taken care of at the proper time" (literally, "at the appropriate hour").

Before the last quarter of the thirteenth century, the most common methods of timekeeping in the monastery as elsewhere were the sundial and the water clock (also known as the *clepsydra*), the latter a device known since at least 1400 B.C.E. Certainly both had disadvantages. The sundial relied on an inconsistent "power source," and was useless at night,[32] and the water clock was prone to freezing, clogging, and the erosion of the mechanism.[33] But, strangely, the principal difficulty with both implements was that they measured equal increments of time.

Throughout this period, the philosophical and practical ideal was a day that was divided into hours of unequal lengths depending on the changing duration of sunlight in the various seasons. Even in pre-Christian times, the tyranny of the sundial was remarked upon since it was out of step with the natural rhythms of life. As one early poet put it:

> The gods confound the man who first found out
> How to distinguish hours. Confound him, too,
> Who in this place set up a sundial,
> To cut and hack my days so wretchedly
> Into small pieces! When I was a boy
> My belly was my sundial—one surer,
> truer, and more exact than any of them.[34]

To create a device that would measure unequal lengths of time accurately proved to be extremely difficult. But even so, there was a strong resistance to accept uniform hours, minutes, and seconds. (Geoffrey Chaucer refers to both systems in his *Treatise on the Astrolabe* [c. 1391], and even as late as 1516 Thomas More still feels the need to defend the use of equal hours in his *Utopia*.)[35] There was seen to be a positive value in maintaining natural rhythms, especially in the monastery, and this value outweighed the inconvenience of having constantly to adjust mechanisms that were unable by themselves to measure time as it was experienced. Indeed, the Benedictine Rule makes provision for the adjustment of the *liturgy* to the variable lengths of night and day when it states that "from Easter till November, the same number of psalms as set down above is to be retained, but on account of the nights being short, no lessons are to be read from the book."[36]

But although this caused the residents of monasteries a certain degree of anxiety about timekeeping,[37] their anxiety about the calendar was greater still, as we have seen, and it would be the work on making the calendar more precise that would force the abandonment of the unequal (or "temporal") hours. And the impetus behind this larger revolution in liturgical time was the invention of the mechanical clock.

From descriptions and reconstructions of machines such as Abbot Richard's *horologium*,[38] it seems that, even though their purpose was to establish an accurate correlation between the motions of the sun, the moon, and the liturgical calendar, they also, as a necessary by-product of their mechanism, marked off increments of time.[39] And it was the popularity of the planetaria that turned the tide in the universal establishment of clock-time:

> Suddenly, towards the middle of the fourteenth century, the mechanical clock seized the imagination of our ancestors. Something of the civic pride which earlier had expended itself in cathedral-building now was diverted to the construction of astronomical clocks of astounding intricacy and elaboration. No European community felt able to hold up its head unless in its midst the planets wheeled in cycles and epicycles, while angels trumpeted, cocks crew, and apostles, kings, and prophets marched and countermarched at the booming of the hours.[40]

And almost overnight, the resistance of the church to a system of timekeeping dictated by mechanical rather than celestial motions collapsed. Clocks began to strike equal hours in city and monastery alike.[41] In 1370, King Charles V decreed that all citizens regulate "their private, commercial, and industrial life to the tempo of the . . . equinoctial hours"[42] and he further ordered all the churches in Paris to ring their tower bells when the official royal clocks struck the hour. (They had previously struck the seven canonical hours only.)[43] Historian of technology Jean Gimpel believes this to have been a watershed in the history of Christian worship:

> By making the churches ring bells at regular, sixty-minute intervals, Charles V was taking a decisive step toward breaking the dominance of the liturgical practices of the Church. The Church would bow to the materialistic practices of the bourgeois and turn its back on eternity.[44]

There is some support for Gimpel's view in the fact that certain groups were particularly reluctant to accept the new technology. In the Greek Orthodox Church, for example, until the twentieth century no mechanical clock was allowed to be installed in a church building. "For them it would have been blasphemy; for them the mechanical division of time into hours, minutes and seconds had no relationship with the eternity of time."[45]

But in the West things were different. As soon as the mechanical clock was invented in the West, it quickly spread not only to the towers of churches, but to their interiors (at first, as we have seen in the case of the abbey church at St. Albans, in the form of astronomical planetaria to demonstrate the "godly order of the cosmos").[46] And soon the entire life of the monasteries, including their prayer life, fell into step with the new technology. Eventually, and certainly by the beginning of the fourteenth century, in all sorts of monastic houses (but perhaps Cistercian houses in particular), clock-regulated liturgy and clock-regulated work functioned interdependently to create the "well-tempered monastery."[47] Oddly enough, whereas the instruments designed to reform the calendar had driven the prayer of the church closer to alignment with the natural rhythms of the celestial world, the legitimate offspring of those instruments, the clock, had driven it further from those same celestial rhythms. "Equal hours," says David Landes, "announced the victory of a new cultural and economic order. Here indeed was an unintended consequence the monks had wrought too well."[48]

In the centuries that followed, the clock not only began to dominate the scheduling of our prayer, our work, and our leisure, but it also became a model and metaphor for great segments of human experience. We spend time and save it and buy it, we feel "run down" or "wound up," our "tickers" go bad, we long to "turn back the clock," and "see the pendulum swing the other way" in sociopolitical matters. Literature and film are filled with warnings about the future of a human race dependent for its existence on the clock. The Lilliputians suggest that Gulliver's watch might be "The God that he worships," and in Samuel Butler's utopian country Erewhon all watches are banned, with serious penalties imposed for possessing one.[49] Day and night, summer and winter, the machine whose "product is seconds and minutes"[50] grinds on. And even the liturgical concern with eternity has been powerless to stop it.

The direct relationship between the clock and the liturgical life of Christians did not confine itself to the ordering of monastic prayer, or to the increasing precedence of civil over ecclesiastical activity.[51] In Western liturgy at least, the dominance of the clock as a determiner of liturgical time is felt everywhere, so that there is almost nothing that will elicit sharper comment from churchgoers than a service of public worship that "runs over the hour." And that dominance has increased with the increase of programmed "God slots" on the radio and on television. Occasionally, a warning is sounded by those with an interest in the deeper rhythms of the liturgy:

> The numbering of years and days, and finally minutes and seconds, may also threaten eternity. . . . If time is numbered, we can no longer escape its undoing by entering ritual's eternity even for a little while, for when we return, we can hardly avoid knowing that our sojourn in ritual lasted for, let us say, an hour and a half on a certain day of a certain month. . . . Number gives eternity, which once informed life and was infused by it, into the hands of death.[52]

The solution to the problems caused by the dominance of the clock is far from clear. Some people call for a return to a "Golden Age," when the rhythms of nature and the rhythms of prayer coincided. But as this brief survey of the history of the clock has demonstrated, that Golden Age is farther back than we usually suppose, and therefore returning to it is less likely than we may think.

CONCLUSION

In this chapter I have examined two different ways in which Christian worship has responded to the challenge of technological change. The first case describes how a deep liturgical need for an accurate calendar was perceived, and how a remedy was clearly identified. But that remedy was a technological one, and its development had overstepped ideological and religious boundaries. As a result, it was ignored for over three centuries by those with the power and authority to implement change. It was easier and safer to live with the problems than rashly to embrace a technological solution that was also tinged with the influence of the "infidel."

The second case describes a quite similar kind of technological development, but a quite different liturgical response. Almost as soon as the mechanical clock was developed, it began to infiltrate the structures and processes of Christian liturgy at every level. (Indeed, so powerful was the image of the clock and the clockmaker, that eventually it would become a dominant theological metaphor for understanding and interpreting the world and God.) No official ecclesiastical judgment was called for, and none was issued. But the influence of the clock on Christian worship has been both profound and pervasive.

Clearly, predictions about how the relationship between liturgy and technology will develop cannot be based solely on the broad characteristics of the technology itself. The mechanical clock that was so firmly embraced by the liturgical system developed directly out of the astronomical devices which were rejected. Each instrument was designed to increase precision in the measurement of time, and the promotion of each was tied to monastic life and practice. Some explanation for the divergent responses may lie in the fact that the *astrolabe* and *rectangulus* were in some sense technologies of the "experts," the mathematicians and astronomers, while the clock very quickly passed into the public domain. In a period of growing trade and a rising merchant class, the need for accurate scheduling increasingly dominated the life of towns and cities, and many people learned to count by the bells of the clock. Not by the old church bells ringing the canonical hours; these did not mark equal units and hence did not lend themselves to addition and subtraction. But the new bells and the calculations they made possible (how long until? how long since?) were a school for all who listened and began to organize their lives around them.[53]

Having become part of the fabric of daily life, the mechanical clock was equally a part of that thread of the fabric which was Christian worship. The impact of astronomical devices, on the other hand, is more conceptual than actual, despite the entertainment value of the elaborate *horlogia*. As compelling and logical as Roger Bacon's treatises on the dating of Easter might have been, they reached only the learned few.

The story of the *astrolabe* and clock, then, is not about the official liturgical rejection or acceptance of technology per se. It is rather about the effect on Christian worship that occurs when a particular technology is popularly received and allowed to penetrate the liturgical life of Christian women and men. At the same time, we can begin to see that the official suspicion of technology in the Middle Ages, which has usually been caricatured as general and indiscriminate, may not run as uniformly through the system as we had previously believed.

FIVE

WORSHIP AND TECHNOLOGY IN HISTORY, 2: LITURGY AND BIOTECHNICS

Biotechnology is a relatively new word.[1] But it describes something that has existed for centuries wherever mechanics and human physiology have been brought together. John Wesley, for example, who like other Anglican clergy of his day provided "amateur medical services to the poor,"[2] was both renowned and ridiculed for his prescription of what we would now call "electroconvulsive therapy" (ECT) for a variety of ills.[3] (His own machine for this purpose is preserved at the Epworth Rectory.) Now, as then, biotechnology is the marriage of a biological theory to a technological process in order that some real or perceived human need might be met.

From the early-nineteenth century onward, one aspect of biotechnology that has had a particularly significant impact on a whole variety of Christian worship practices—namely, the various technological responses to disease and to theories of disease. And while such prosaic matters as hygiene, sanitation, food preservation, and public health administration may seem to be far from the concern of those interested in public prayer, it is precisely these matters that must be taken seriously when investigating the history of technology as a liturgical change-agent.

THE BIOTECHNOLOGY OF FUNERALS

At the beginning of the nineteenth century, the presence of noxious gases and effluents called "miasmas" had become firmly established as the prevailing explanation for disease contagion.[4] In his 1827 treatise on malaria, for example, John Macculloch says with conviction, "It has long been familiar to physicians that there is produced by marshes and swamps a poisonous and aeroform substance, the cause, not only of ordinary fevers, but of intermittents; and to this unknown agent of disease the term *marsh miasma* has been applied."[5]

But swamplands were not the only source of harmful miasmas. Theoretically, they could emanate from any material in the process of decomposition, and particularly from human and animal remains. Because the progressive popularity of the miasmatic theory of disease paralleled almost exactly the progressive overcrowding of town and city graveyards, those concerned with public health began to look to the church burial ground as a probable source of miasmatic discharge.

During the previous century, in both Britain and in the United States, as well as on the European continent, the general condition of churchyard cemeteries had seriously deteriorated. The situation in England typifies the problem. There, the graveyard in the parish church had been since Anglo Saxon times the presumed place of burial for every person resident in the parish precincts, unless one were wealthy enough to own a private chapel or to be interred in the church building itself. But after a thousand years of such burials, (and especially with the rapid rise in population in the eighteenth century) something of a saturation point had been reached, and particularly in the cities.[6]

Contemporary descriptions of the conditions that prevailed are uncommonly gruesome, with abundant images of bodies stacked and jumbled together, and of the collapse of churchyard walls, which resulted in corpses in various states of decay spilling out onto adjacent streets.[7]

During epidemics of cholera or influenza there were indescribable scenes at churchyards, with the ground looking like a ploughed field, queues of mourners miserably waiting their turn, and navvies hired as extras on the coffins.[8]

Although there were periodic calls for burial reform during the years around the turn of the nineteenth century, it was the great cholera epidemics of the 1830s and 1840s that would force a solution to this problem.[9] The presence of corpses exuding noxious miasmas in areas of dense population was overwhelmingly seized upon as an explanation for the spread of the disease, and the burial of the dead moved quickly and surely from being a primarily *religious* to being a primarily *political* and *biotechnic* concern. In a parody of Thomas Gray's *Elegy in a Country Churchyard* (1751), the satirical magazine *Punch* offered its editorial opinion of the situation:

> Full many a gas of direst power unclean,
> The dark o'erpeopled graves of London bear
> Full many a poison, born to kill unseen,
> And spread its rankness in the neighboring air.[10]

At the same time, very similar conditions prevailed in the various parts of the United States, and official committees were charged with the task of assessing the overcrowding of cemeteries and providing solutions. In 1842, the New York City Board of Health established such a committee, which recommended that "intermural" (inner city) cemeteries be prohibited, and suggested that the existing city cemeteries be converted into parks "instead of remaining receptacles of putrifying matter and hot-beds of miasma."[11]

In England, alternative locations for burial had been tried from around the turn of the nineteenth century, but these early experiments were mainly a part of the Nonconformist response to Anglican monopoly on burials.

> Nonconformist ministers were not allowed to conduct burials in the parish churchyard, and the parish priest, even if not so inclined, was obliged by law to read the full Anglican burial service over the dissenting dead. In thousands of parishes throughout England and Wales at least, the sole recourse for burial was to the parish churchyard.[12]

In addition to the religious incongruity of saying an Anglican service over the body of a pious Nonconformist, there was also the matter of the burial fee. The members of the Free Churches not only had to endure the indignity of being forced to submit to the Anglican funeral rites, but also had to pay the parish clergy a fee for the privilege![13]

But the alternative locations for graveyards that were chosen in these early days were mainly adjacent to Nonconformist chapels, which were themselves very often tucked away in inconspicuous locations for reasons of security, and with little surrounding space for burials. While this represented a beginning,[14] it gave little real relief to the serious and pervasive burial problems of the time. And so, propelled by the fear of disease, by the growing dissatisfaction, in England and Wales at least, with the degree of Anglican control over the rites of death, and by the popular disgust (fueled by the media) with the condition of urban burial sites, a new movement was born: the suburban park cemetery. The final stanza in *Punch*'s editorial poem makes the case nicely:

> No longer seek Corruption to enclose
> Within the places of mankind's abode;
> But far from cities let our dust repose
> Where daisies blossom on the verdant clod.[15]

The place of Christian burial soon became a key element in the technology of sanitation, a biotechnological weapon in its own right. Parklike cemeteries such as Mount Auburn in Massachusetts (which contemporary commentators referred to as "a dormitory for the deceased"), Kensal Green, Highgate, and Brompton in suburban London, the Glasgow Necropolis, and Père Lachaise outside of Paris[16] were planned and developed well away from centers of population, and each had as its focal point a cemetery chapel from which funerals might be conducted.[17] An excursion by train, sometimes lasting an hour or more, began to be necessary for the funeral party, and the station platform became both the physical and psychological starting place for the ritualization of mourning.[18] Although Bishop Charles Blomfield of London predicted in 1847 that people would resist attending funerals by train, he was mistaken. Within a few decades, the "respectable funeral" became the aspiration of persons of all classes, and a vast array of manuals detailing proper "funeral etiquette" were available for consultation. As Ruth

Richardson says: "The funeral came to be the rite of passage par excellence in which to assert financial and social position—a sort of secular last judgment."[19] All of this was stage-managed by fashionable firms of funeral directors, and the control of the church over the rites of death was further reduced.[20]

Finally, beginning in the late-1840s, a variety of laws restricting traditional burial practices were passed. Most followed the pattern of the "Metropolitan Interments Act" passed by Parliament in 1850,[21] which stipulated that no body was to be buried in an urban churchyard cemetery or within two hundred yards of a dwelling. The Church of England fought strenuously against this Act, fearing (rightly) that their monopoly on burial fees would be broken. (The closing of a churchyard could cost a clergyman up to £700 per year in lost burial fees.) But in the end the Church was forced to comply with the Act, and as a result between 1852 and 1862 over 4000 urban and town churchyards in England were closed.[22] The move from churchyard to cemetery was well on its way to being completed.[23]

Several changes in the official ritual of burial resulted from the removal of the gravesite from the immediate vicinity of the church. The most immediate consequence was the breakdown of the intimate relationship between funeral and burial rites that had existed (in peacetime at least) throughout most of Christian history. As intricate as the early-medieval rites of death were, "the character of these early rites . . . is the clear incorporation of the necessary stages of burial into a liturgical pattern."[24] By the time of the Reformation, the ritual included a procession from the house of the deceased to the church, the office of the dead, the funeral mass, the procession to the grave, and the burial.

Although all of the sixteenth-century Continental reformers sought to simplify the medieval rites of death, they nevertheless maintained the cohesion between funeral and burial. In many of the rites the entire service took place at the graveside.[25] The first rites for the Church of England are very similar, even though they share in the overall conservatism of Cranmer's reform, and there were few major changes in the form and structure of the burial rites in the successive sixteenth- and seventeenth-century editions. In the 1662 *Book of Common Prayer*, for example, the rubrical directions state:

The Priest and Clerks meeting the corpse at the entrance of the Church-yard, and going before it, either into the Church, or towards the grave, shall say. . . .

And although various parts of the service that follow are appointed to be read "after they are come into the Church" or "when they come to the grave," one is still left with the clear impression that the funeral and burial rites comprise a single liturgical unity, and that the rubrics simply represent a bit of "stage-managing" within that unity.[26]

But as the separation between the church and the gravesite becomes more fixed in the liturgical imagination, the rubrical and euchological specificity about both the funeral and burial increases:

The new cemeteries were so far away that it was no longer possible for the [funeral] procession to accompany the body from the home to the church and from the church to the cemetery without interruption. The ceremony had to be divided into two stages: first from the home to the church and next from the church to the cemetery.[27]

And so, for example, in the *Book of Common Prayer* as proposed in 1928 to replace the 1662 edition, the service has been clearly divided in two, with sections marked "The Service in Church" and "The Burial."[28] By 1980, the *Alternative Service Book* has designated two quite distinct ritual elements: "The Funeral" and "The Committal."

During the period in question, this sort of fragmentation of the rites of death came to be embodied in the liturgical books of all denominations. A sampling of the Methodist *Disciplines* from 1824 to 1950 reveals the progressive breakdown of the integrity of the rites of death, manifested by an increase in the amount of liturgical material that is specified for use in the church and at the grave respectively. In 1824 three short sentences from Scripture are provided for use as the minister meets the corpse,[29] and the rest of the funeral service takes place at the gravesite itself. Eighty years later, in 1904, two psalms and an Epistle lesson are added to the 1820 readings,[30] and the rubric specifies that, "In the House or Church may be read one or both of the following psalms, or some other suitable portion of the Holy Scripture." An expanded version of the 1820 service is then said "at the grave, when the Corpse is laid in the earth." By 1956, however, a whole series of readings and prayers running to eight pages of text are offered before prayers are said "at the grave, when the people are assembled." Funeral and burial services are quite clearly distinct and separate entities. The most recent Roman Catholic *Order of Funerals* gives the fragmentation of the rites of death a new status and authority, offering as it does a whole range of interchangeable options for the ordering of funeral and burial rites individually.[31]

But there are also deeper, experiential changes that result from the removal of the graveyard from the immediate vicinity of the church, changes that effect what might be called the "liturgical spirituality" of every worshiper at every service. The difference can be illuminated by looking at the argument for churchyard burials given by Charles Wheatley in his influential commentary on the *Prayer Book* (1710):

> Everyone that could pay for the honour [of being buried in the church building] has generally been allowed it: but since all cannot pay, nor churches contain all, there is a necessity of providing other conveniences for this use. And this has generally been done . . . by inclosing some of the ground round the church, for a burying place or a churchyard; that so, as the faithful are going to the house of prayer, they may be brought to a fit temper and disposition of mind, by a prospect of the graves and monuments of their friends: nothing being more apt to raise our devotion than serious thoughts upon death and mortality.[32]

The removal of the funeral to a building, such as a mortuary chapel, within which no other sort of religious service takes place, and the removal of the gravesite to a location far away from the precincts of the church, depletes a fund of theological and communal images and severely reduces the sense described so powerfully by Wheatley that the living and the dead are a part of one "holy communion."[33] As one modern commentator says, "Our memories are no longer anchored to a locality, and with cemeteries removed from worship-places, some sense of the communion of saints living and departed is lost."[34] Where Wheatley saw the churchyard as an occasion for doctrinal insight and development among those who would be worshiping weekly in the church building which stood within it, for "serious thoughts upon death and mortality," the new suburban cemeteries were designed to be catalysts for moral uplift and esthetic improvement for the general populace. In his treatise on the *Laying-out, Planting, and Managing of Cemeteries* (1843), landscape architect and entrepreneur J. C. Louden argues that, in addition to the promotion of public health and disease control, "A secondary object is, or ought to be, the improvement of the moral sentiments and general taste of all classes and more especially of the great masses of society."[35] By the end of the nineteenth century, the suburban-garden cemetery had become a fashionable destination for excursion parties, where rare and interesting botanical specimens could be viewed along well-designed pathways, where the human sensibilities were managed by the creation of picturesque "vistas," and where, surrounded by memorials to the dead, the living were provided with an environment saturated with high-Victorian sentimental and moralistic piety.

The new dignified and landscaped cemeteries served many purposes: providing a setting in which the grief of the bereaved could be expressed and assuaged in monument and verse; a setting also in which the wealthy could assert through prominently sited and imposing monuments the influence they had exerted in life; and finally as a source of "rational recreation."[36]

At the same time, official liturgical texts themselves moved away from the idea that the funeral was intended to remind the living of "the inevitability of death, of the need to prepare for it, and of resurrection, judgment, and eternal life."[37] It is a long way, spiritually and liturgically, from

> Man that is born of a woman hath but a short time to live, and is full of misery. He cometh up, and is cut down like a flower: he fleeth as it were a shadow. In the midst of life we are in death: of who may we seek succor, but of thee, O Lord, who for our sins are most justly displeased?

to

> God of love, we thank you for all with which you have blessed us even to this day: for the gift of joy in days of health and strength, and for the gifts of your abiding presence and promise in days of pain and grief. We praise you for home and friends, and for our

baptism and place in your church with all who have faithfully lived and died.[38]

In addition, the progressive, parallel development of the funeral industry, with its own technological arsenal—embalming, refrigeration, cremation—further removed the rites of death and burial from the Christian liturgical center. Not only has the increasing "professionalization of death" taken over many aspects of the funeral that had previously been centered in and around the church (both in the sense of the building and the local Christian community), but it has also disturbed a whole range of paraliturgical activities surrounding the death of a Christian. By the end of the First World War, that is within fifty years from the time the undertaker began to function and be regarded as a funeral director, a whole range of traditional household mourning rites had largely disappeared. These rites had closely followed local and regional patterns, and had included such emotionally and ritually satisfying practices as laying-out, watching, shroud-weaving, waking, sin-eating, and viewing. Since these were almost always performed and presided over by women (and skills in this area were often passed on from mother to daughter), their loss becomes a part of the story of the increasing defeminization of Christian worship that has taken place during the last century.[39]

Clearly, the biotechnology of disease control which developed more than a century and a half ago continues to exert a powerful influence on contemporary rites of death. Peter Jupp argues that "whilst the connection between burial, disease, hygiene and sanitation did not fit in every case, the connection became embedded in most people's minds" during this period.[40] In addition, clergy experience an increasing loss of control over the rites of death. As Roman Catholic priest Robert Hovda laments:

> It is very difficult to understand how American funerals got to be as pretentious and ostentatious, as phony and unreal and camouflaged, as destructive of the economic well-being of low-to-moderate income families as they have become. . . . The rites of the church are being smothered, thrown back into the shadows by a combination of cultural practices that militate against the healthy and spiritual values of simplicity, honesty, and prudent economy.[41]

The sense that the Christian rites of death have been "hijacked" by a high-tech funeral industry is strong.[42] But popular opinion also contributes to holding the Christian funeral on its present course. Recent efforts to restore the funeral to the church building, or to include the provision of columbaria or cemetery space in new church plans most often meet with deep resistance on the part not only of clergy and laity, but of public health officials and legislators as well.[43]

THE BIOTECHNOLOGY OF COMMUNION

The miasma theory of disease prevailed throughout the first three-quarters of the nineteenth century, and was only gradually usurped by the discovery of a new disease agent: the microbe. If the biotechnology of disease management founded on the miasmic theory had a significant impact on the rites of death, then germ theory, both on its own and in league with a particular strategy for social control, permanently changed the face of the Protestant communion service.

This time, however, disease control and sanitation were to serve only as the handmaidens of a wider sociopolitical movement. During the middle part of the century, temperance, and particularly Christian temperance, had gained momentum until it dominated the agenda of both political parties and churches, and not only in the United States but in the British Isles as well.[44] In a series of sermons on temperance in 1826, the influential pastor and preacher Lyman Beecher (1775–1863) put the case most forcefully:

> Who can estimate the hatred of God, of his Word and worship . . . which [drink] occasions? How many thousands does it detain every Sabbath-day from the house of God—cutting them off from the means of grace and hardening them against their efficacy?[45]

The original aim of the Temperance Movement was the reform of drunkards and the limitation of the hours that saloons could engage in the sale of liquor.[46] But soon a strong emphasis on teetotalism was established,[47] until by the mid-1840s abstaining from alcohol was advanced as the most reasonable and obvious solution to the increasing social problems of the day: homelessness, poverty, crime, and mental illness.[48] The politics of this more strenuous version of Temperance quickly became a dominant force in the American cultural agenda, and in 1919 the near-total prohibition of the manufacture and sale of alcohol was enforced under the Nineteenth Amendment to the United States Constitution.[49]

Almost as soon as total abstinence became a regular feature of the Temperance platform, the question of communion wine arose. For many the answer was inevitable:

> Shall we use [unfermented wine] as sacramental wine, or shall we cling to the drunkard's cup, and thus set an example which has encouraged, and is encouraging, many a member to travel the broad road which has led and will continue to lead to so many sorrows and woes untold and finally to a drunkard's grave and a drunkard's future?[50]

But many Christian supporters of the original aims of the Temperance Movement found that the call for teetotalism to extend to the Lord's Supper was too radical a step, and distanced themselves from the Movement. Within individual denominations schisms resulted in some places, dividing those congregations who continued to use fermented wine at communion and those who did not.[51] In the end, the impact of teetotalism on the liturgy "produced a lasting controversy over the use of wine at Communion services and ramified into a dispute over the use and interpretation of the Bible."[52]

In 1830, alcoholic wine was used in every communion service of every denomination, so the teetotal pledge threatened widespread disruption. But although the ideological shift from moderation to total abstinence was a rapid one, the progress toward a liquor-free communion service was quite slow; by 1840, five years after the New York State Temperance Society had endorsed teetotalism, only 7 percent of congregations in New York offered unfermented wine at the Lord's Supper.[53] The cause of the delay was in part due to the considerable debate over the biblical basis of such a change in the traditional eucharistic elements.[54] But more important, there were serious practical difficulties in providing unfermented wine in any large quantities, difficulties that only advances in biotechnology would solve.

A look at the progress of communion temperance in the Methodist Episcopal Church gives some indication of the situation. While

Methodists were widely sympathetic to the Temperance Movement in other ways,[55] it was not until after the Civil War that the minutes of the various Methodist Conferences began to record calls for the provision of alternatives to alcoholic wine for the Lord's Supper.[56] The New York East Annual Conference, for example, in its 1869 "Report on Temperance," says cautiously:

> 2d. The Sacramental use of intoxicating wine is often attended with serious danger to those whose appetite for stimulants is only held in abeyance by a rigid course of total abstinence: therefore the expediency and even the rightfulness of such use should be carefully considered.[57]

But within three years, much of the tentativeness about communion alcohol had disappeared among American Methodists. In 1872, the New York Annual Conference passed the following Resolution:

> *Whereas:* The use of intoxicating, that is, fermented wines in our communion service, is incompatible with the teachings of the Word of God and the example of our Lord Jesus Christ. . . . *Therefore resolved:* That we will exert ourselves to the utmost to secure the general introduction of unfermented wine for Sacramental purposes in all our charges.[58]

In that same year, the General Conference minutes record a resolution which recommends "the use of unfermented wine on our sacramental occasions."[59]

What must be noted, however, is that despite their certainty that the use of fermented wine is "incompatible with the teachings of the Word of God," there is the invariable suggestion in these resolutions that unfermented communion wine will be difficult to procure, and that therefore its use can only be "recommended" (or "earnestly recommended") rather than required.[60] And indeed it was difficult to procure. It would take the biotechnic revolution born with the fermentation studies of Louis Pasteur (1822–95) for nonalcoholic wines to be widely available for sacramental use.

Having begun his work in 1857 on the fermentation of lactic acid in milk, Pasteur became interested in the processes by which yeasts grow and produce alcohol in beer (1860).[61] In quick succession followed the development of the microbe theory of diseases, immunology, and food sterilization.[62] The biotechnological consequences of Pasteur's work were enormous:

> It was only with the knowledge that microorganisms are the active agents of organic chemical change that one could begin to understand the role of microbes in nature and learn to prevent their harmful activities or manipulate their beneficial activities.[63]

From the very beginning these two sets of discoveries—the microbe as an agent of beneficial fermentation and the microbe as an agent of putrefaction and disease—went hand in hand. And while biotechnological responses to both discoveries would affect the practice of communion in different ways, all of the changes that resulted can be traced directly back to Pasteur.

Pasteur's own studies in the fermentation of wine did not begin until 1863.[64] His experimental efforts to prevent wine spoilage (what we would now call the "pasteurization" of wine)[65] were extended to beer in 1866, and within a few years his techniques for the management of fermentation were being publicized in America as well. And it was in America that the new techniques for preventing spoilage were first applied to inhibiting the fermentation of grape juice for the purpose of making nonalcoholic communion wine.

In his 1872 treatise "Communion Wine and Bible Temperance," the Reverend James W. Townsend, having spent nearly one hundred pages setting forth various philological and biblical arguments for the prohibition of fermented wine at communion,[66] turns to a description of his own efforts to develop suitable quantities of unfermented wine for eucharistic consumption. Townsend notes the activities of Pasteur,[67] and records his various attempts to replicate Pasteur's results using grape juice. Townsend also devised his own experimental methods for inhibiting fermentation, including boiling, filtering, adding sulfur, holding casks under water, and suspending bottles in various locations. These experiments cannot be said to be unreservedly successful:

> Of the four bottles which I suspended in my well, two of which I have not given account of were suspended by small strings which decayed and the bottles are supposed to be at the bottom of the well. . . . Of the two bottles placed in the Cold Room, I brought one

into my office, intending to take it to my home, but after standing in the warm office for a few hours, it burst.[68]

But Townsend declares that the fourth bottle contained unspoiled, unfermented grape juice suitable for use as communion wine. It was a beginning, if a hesitant one, and Townsend says that he hopes by his example "to encourage all who grow grapes to manufacture or preserve unfermented wine, instead of fermented," and that they "need not be discouraged or unnecessarily disappointed in their first attempts at preserving unfermented wines."[69]

It would take the labors of a devout Methodist layperson to make the extended use of unfermented wine at communion a reality. Dr. Thomas Bramwell Welch, an ardent Temperance supporter, worked diligently toward the application of Pasteur's milk sterilization techniques to fruit juices, with the clear intention of providing an unfermented grape juice for use at communion.[70] Having abandoned his work as a lay preacher because of a weak throat, Welch studied medicine and worked first as a physician and then as a dentist, promoting his own line of patent elixirs.[71] But, it was his appointment as a Communion Steward in Vineland, New York, which would redirect his experimental energy:

> Unfermented grape juice was born in 1869 out of a passion to serve God by helping His Church to give its communion "the fruit of the vine," instead of the "cup of devils."[72]

Welch's son Charles Edgar, himself influenced by frustrated missionary zeal,[73] promoted his family's product widely in the Protestant churches beginning in the late-1870s as a way of extending Temperance principles to the practice of Holy Communion. One advertisement read:

> If your druggist hasn't the kind that was used in Galilee containing not a particle of alcohol, write to us for prices.[74]

Another argued that:

> Churches will find Welch's grape juice as economical as fermented wine, and certainly the preference should be given to the pure and harmless, even though the price were a little more.[75]

So while in the *Ritual* rubrics for communion in 1876 Conference could only *recommend* "the use of pure, unfermented juice of the grape on sacramental occasions" (p. 270), four years later in 1880 that recommendation could become a demand: "Let none but the pure, unfermented juice of the grape be used in administering the Lord's Supper" (p. 284). (However, there is still included the loophole clause "wherever practicable.") Finally, in 1916, the *Discipline* is unequivocal: "Let the pure, unfermented juice of the grape be used in administering the Lord's Supper" (p. 401). And of course, Temperance-minded Baptists, Presbyterians, Disciples of Christ, and Congregationalists followed suit.[76]

Not only did the practical application of pasteurization technology to grape juice profoundly change the eucharistic practice of wide segments of American and British Protestantism (and of those whom they evangelized throughout the world), but it also had serious implications for ecumenism as well. The early temperance campaign had divided roughly along denominational lines, with what historian Richard Jensen has called the "pietists" (that is Methodists, Presbyterians, Baptists, and Scandinavian Lutherans) generally on one side of the question and the "liturgicals" (Roman Catholics, Episcopalians, and German Lutherans) on the other.[77] The issue of fermented communion wine divided along exactly the same lines and combined with the more generalized anti-Catholic sentiments of the period to fix a barrier to intercommunion that was more potent than doctrine.[78]

The question of fermented versus unfermented wine, while largely settled within individual denominations by the first decade of the twentieth century, continues to create divisions within the Body of Christ. One example will suffice. In 1965 the Convocations of the Church of England and the British Methodist Conference gave conditional acceptance to various proposals for the organic, institutional union of the two churches and in 1968 began to make preparations for what was referred to as Stage One of the reunion scheme. A draft service for reconciliation and an ordinal were prepared, but the question of the use of unfermented wine at communion was one of the major unresolved issues that was remitted to a separate committee for settlement before Stage One could be entered into. In the preliminary report,[79] the question of fermented communion wine is described as "a particularly difficult matter"[80] since the relevant statutes within the Canon Law of the two churches were in direct contradiction. While Methodists were not insisting that Anglicans use unfermented wine, Anglicans were less tolerant, and even the suggestion that fermented wine with the alcohol removed afterwards (described in the Report as "a comparatively new process")[81] might be acceptable was not met with real enthusiasm. The Report stated:

> It would be a tragedy if this issue prevented or marred our coming together. Each Church must be willing, for the sake of the greater good, to begin Stage One by respecting the usages of the other; thus leaving the way open for the continuing amicable debate that is necessary before Stage Two.[82]

It is difficult to assess the degree to which the question of fermented communion wine contributed to the ultimate disintegration of the Unity Scheme in 1970. Suffice it to say that even the plans for Services of Reconciliation, of which communion was an integral component, were halted by the inability of the two churches to come to a common mind on acceptable eucharistic elements. Until the very end, the question of unfermented communion wine is routinely cited as an "unresolved issue" in the reports.

Hygienic Communion

But Pasteur's germ theory and the concomitant development of sterilization techniques for the prevention of spoilage and disease would have a further impact on the practice of communion, this time not only in the Free Churches, but across the denominational spectrum. Spawned by the popular enthusiasm for seeing microbes as the cause of all human ills, the "Personal Hygiene Movement" grew in influence during the first three decades of the twentieth century, but especially after the First World War.[83] The prevention of microbial contact became a goal in all areas of human life, including Christian worship. Individual cups for the sanitary distribution of communion wine, first patented in the United States in 1894, became a standard ecclesiastical accessory.[84] Soon, other devices to aid in the provision of a more hygienic communion were designed and distributed. In the 1934 Eugene McCoy Company's church goods catalogue (whose clientele were mainly Roman Catholics) an item called a "hostainer" appears: "An altar dispenser which is sanitary, rapid, and symbolic. No tweezers, spoons or fingers are used, simply slide the knob and one host drops into the ciborium. Hygienic and liturgically correct. Each: $30.00."[85]

Biotechnological issues continue to arise in the eucharistic life of the Christian churches, and especially as we confront the challenge of HIV infection and AIDS. With the wealth of liturgical scholarship that attended the Second Vatican Council, Christians of all denominations began to recognize the deep symbolic value of the use of a common chalice at the Lord's Supper as a sign of their common unity in the life of Christ. Not only did many Protestant Christians who had moved to individual communion cups earlier in the century return to the ancient custom of the single chalice, but Roman Catholics began to be allowed to receive the eucharistic wine from a common chalice for the first time in centuries.[86] At the very same time, however, both the spread of the AIDS epidemic and the more general fear of infectious disease have put the use of the chalice as a way of dispensing communion wine under serious threat.[87] As long as the fear of infection from a common chalice remains real for many Christians in general, and as long as the possibility of infection from a common chalice remains real for those Christians whose immune systems are impaired by the HIV virus, all pastoral-liturgical arguments for the appropriateness of a common chalice will be of secondary importance. In the end, it may very well be that specifically technological responses to these sorts of challenges will be shaping the liturgical life of the Christian church of the future.

CONCLUSION

We have focused fairly narrowly in this chapter on particular aspects of biotechnology, sanitation, and hygiene and have shown how biotechnic processes made possible (if not inevitable) dramatic changes in certain elements of Christian public prayer. As we saw was the case with the calendar in the previous chapter, the process of liturgical change was set in motion by a perceived need, but here the need was not primarily liturgical, but social and physiological. The resulting ritual and theological shifts in both the communion and funeral services continue to affect wide segments of American Christianity. In addition, some of these changes have also had serious and persistent ecumenical implications.

But clearly it is not enough simply to draw a single line-of-influence from technology to Christian worship. We have also seen how the liturgy itself became caught up in the war against disease as a weapon in the biotechnological arsenal. The actual, clinical success of the sanitary funeral and the sanitary communion in limiting contagion may never be known. But the intention surely was and is to exploit elements of Christian ritual for the reduction of opportunities for infection. And so in the same way we have seen that the history of technology can become absorbed into the history of liturgy, here we see how the history of liturgy can become absorbed into the history of technology.

C H A P T E R
S I X

LITURGY AND MECHANIZATION

Not the external and physical alone is now managed by machinery, but the internal and spiritual also. . . . The same habit regulates not our modes of action alone, but our modes of thought and feeling. Men are grown mechanical in head and heart, as well as in hand. They have lost faith in individual endeavours, and in natural force, of any kind. Not for internal perfection but for external combinations and arrangements for institutions, constitutions, for Mechanism of one sort or another, do they hope and struggle.[1]

This is Thomas Carlyle's complaint: that human beings have become machinelike, and society has taken on a mechanical quality in all of its operations and aspirations. The machine model—of society, of mind, of work, of the human person—has had a pervasive influence on Western consciousness since its beginnings in the scientific rationalism of the seventeenth and eighteenth centuries.[2] Although such a model is only one element within a whole constellation of attitudes, images, and presuppositions that technology both binds and legitimates, it has been a powerful one. Karl Marx observed that the process of mechanized production creates not only an object fit for a particular human subject, but also creates the human subject itself,[3] and social-analyst Lewis Mumford took that one step further in his concept of the "Megamachine," an amalgamation of persons and things that function together toward the efficient performance of given tasks.[4] The more we look, the more we see the extent to which we ourselves have been molded to fit the world of technological artifacts, and the more we can see that the "myth of the machine" can stand as representative of the larger technological worldview. As Mumford says, for much of recent human history:

> The machine . . . not merely served as the ideal model for explaining and eventually controlling all organic activities, but its wholesale fabrication and its continued improvement were what alone could give meaning to human existence.[5]

In the beginning, it was thought that actual physiological changes would have to take place in human beings in order that they might be compatible with the machines that were increasingly part of the human habitat. When Georges Claudin arrived in Paris in 1865, he found a great city, crisscrossed by railways and trams, illuminated with artificial lighting, and filled with the sights and sounds of commercial manufacturing. He begins his famous description of the city with the observation that the recent technological discoveries have the tendency to "bend our senses and our organs in such a way that causes us to believe that our physical and moral constitution is no longer in rapport with them." Science and technology, he claims, have made a world that the human being is not suited to inhabit. "We should like to venture into it," Claudin says wistfully, "but it does not take us long to recognize that it requires a constitution we lack and organs we do not have."[6] While few believe that the radical changes in human physiology suggested by Claudin have actually taken place in the succeeding years,[7] most would agree that there have been certain psychological and perceptual changes that have allowed contemporary men and women to live comfortably in a technological society. In order to "venture into" the world technology has made, we have had to see ourselves as being, in some substantial and integrated way, part of it.

Many recent commentators, however, suggest that the machine model is beginning to lose some of its influence, and that loss of influence is one of the hallmarks of postmodernity. They cite the rise of service-based economy, Green politics and theology, New Age religious movements, and a growing pessimism about the limits of technology as evidence for a shift toward a more organic worldview. But this argument is by no means universally accepted, and even its supporters would agree that any such shift in perception is in its very early stages and that the "myth of the machine" continues to retain much of its power in the corporate consciousness of the industrialized West.[8] (For example urban sociologists John Logan and Harvey Motoloch can still confidently call the contemporary city a "Growth Machine" and say that "the growth machine coalition mobilizes . . . cultural motivations, legitimizes them and channels them into activities that are consistent with growth goals.")[9] Whatever the current status of the "myth of the machine," any analysis of the impact of technological thinking on those who worship will be incomplete without taking the mechanical paradigm into account. At the very least, it can provide us with a model for thinking about the way in which a given conceptual framework can influence the liturgical life of individuals and communities.

What specific issues does the "myth of the machine" raise for students of worship as they reflect on the ways in which contemporary men and women and children approach Christian ritual? How do people enmeshed (to a greater or lesser degree) in this particular context perceive the liturgical process in which they are engaging? Rather than look at all of the various facets of the machine paradigm in attempting to answer these questions, it may be useful to isolate and give attention to a limited number of particular features that have direct relevance to the study of Christian worship: the quest for the elimination of "play" (in the sense of increasingly small tolerances), progressive perfectibility, componentiality, and the reliance on expertise.

The Quest for the Elimination of "Play" and Progressive Perfectibility

In both simple and sophisticated machines, an elimination of play is considered essential to the smooth and efficient functioning of the device. Quite simply, the component parts must fit, and fit precisely. In the early stages of the Industrial Age, it was almost universally believed that one would eventually reduce tolerances to zero in all parts of the machine, and that perpetual motion (first proposed, it is thought, by Villard de Honnecourt in 1235)[10] was a reasonable goal. One eighteenth-century engineer observed:

Whoever seeks from power more work than is produced so far by our calculus or theory of mechanics, is in fact seeking the *Perpetuum mobile* and will not find it. . . . He must know what sort of theory is most important or in what manner he can arrive at it, *namely by the avoidance of friction.*[11]

One important by-product of this quest for the elimination of play is the notion of progressive perfectibility: the view that in time and under the right circumstances one progresses toward a machine perfectly suited to its task. While the immediate expectation of a better world overall may no longer be the experience of large numbers of the population, the belief that material objects and the systems that produce them are inherently "improvable" is still very much part of the American consciousness. (For decades the advertising industry has relied on this popular conviction, and "new and improved" has been an almost indispensable description for each change in product design.) But the idea of progressive perfectibility has not been confined to artifacts and modes of production; it has applied equally to various kinds of social institutions as well—governments, systems of education, workplaces, families.

Even the arts and nature have been discussed in terms of the elimination of play and progressive perfectibility. As long ago as 1831, John Stuart Mill wrote in the *Westminster Review*:

It would be a pity that poetry should be an exception to the Great Law of progress that attains in human affairs: and it is not. The machinery of a poem is not less susceptible of improvement than the machinery of a cotton mill; nor is there any better reason why the one should retrograde from the days of Milton than the other from those of Arkwright.[12]

The presence in almost every American city and town of "Arts Improvement Societies" beginning in the 1920s is a popular manifestation of this sense of the "Great Law of progress" working toward the elimination of "play" in the machinery of the various art forms. "A hope has grown stronger with the experience of each year," wrote the architect Frank Lloyd Wright in 1901, amounting now to a gradually deepening conviction:

In the Machine lies the only future of art and craft, and, as I believe, a glorious future; that the Machine is, in fact, the metamorphosis of ancient art and craft; that we are at last face to face with the Machine: the modern Sphinx.[13]

The natural world has been equally subject to this kind of analysis. For most of the nineteenth century, machine technology was systematically applied to the task of molding nature into the shape and function that God somehow failed to give it in the first instance. "The cosmic freedom of the natural phenomenon," writes one late-nineteenth-century enthusiast for waterwheels, "becomes transformed by the machine into an order and law that outside forces of an ordinary kind are unable to disrupt."[14] Everything from landscape design to the selective breeding of domestic animals can be interpreted as a development of this idea that human technological intervention can improve the natural world. Genetic engineering is simply the contemporary manifestation of an attitude that is over a century old.

Clearly this sense that nature can be perfected by the intervention of technology spills over into the idea that the human person is itself also perfectible by the same means. Already by the turn of the twentieth century it was widely believed that progressive human improvement will happen through natural processes. In his *Notebooks* (1919) the utopian satirist Samuel Butler, for example, had written:

Give the world time, an infinite number of epochs, and according to its past and present system, like the coming tide each epoch will advance on each, but so slowly that it can hardly be traced, man's body becoming finer to bear his finer mind, till man becomes not only an angel but an archangel.[15]

This kind of utopian sentiment, combined with appeals to popular versions of Darwinism and Lamarckism, made human psychological, physiological, and spiritual perfectibility a part of the more general belief in progress, which characterizes this period. More recently, many observers have viewed the growth of such things as pop psychology, cryogenics, cosmetic surgery, and experimental genetics as clear indications of the marketing power harnessed by the ideal of progressive human improvement in the late-twentieth century. And so it is difficult to argue successfully that we can place liturgy outside the quest for progressive perfectibility and the elimination of play by arguing that it is a "natural phenomenon," part of the natural human drive to seek out and worship the divine. The "myth of the machine" is operative here as well.

RELIGION AND HUMAN PERFECTIBILITY

> Praise God for the harvest of science and skill,
> The urge to discover, create and fulfill.
> For all new inventions that promise to gain
> A future more hopeful, a world more humane.[16]

By the mid-nineteenth century, various forms of religion had come to be firmly allied to the progressive improvement of society, and not only to its moral improvement, but its economic and technical improvement as well. During certain periods (notably the years between the Civil War and the First World War, the late-1920s to the mid-1930s, and the 1960s) the coalition between religion and the quest for an end to child labor, drunkenness, slavery, racism, torture, unjust war, and political persecution established the ideal of measurable moral improvement. The historian of nineteenth-century Christianity Timothy L. Smith describes the kind of optimistic enthusiasm that pervaded American religion in the period:

> "The grand feature of our times is that *all* is *Progress*," exulted the editors of the *Independent* in 1851. Christianity and culture seemed to be marching together "onward and upward" toward the "grand consummation of prophecy in a civilized, an enlightened and a sanctified world" and the establishment of "that spiritual kingdom which God has ordained shall triumph and endure."[17]

One particular religious movement has special relevance for our study of the relationship between Christian worship and technological thinking. This is Revivalism, associated with frontier camp meetings and open-air "protracted meetings" in the nineteenth century, and with fervent tabernacle-type preaching in both urban and rural settings in the 1920s and 1930s. The principles of revivalism were founded on the notion of a Christian commitment:

> Not merely to preach the gospel to every creature, but to reorganize human society in accordance with the law of God. To abolish all corruptions in religion and all abuses in the social system and, so far as it has been erected on false principles, to take it down and erect it anew.[18]

Revivalism spread down the Erie Canal, completed in 1825 (itself a symbol of the burgeoning industrialization and progressive improvement of the country)[19] and aimed at the redemption and sanctification of America. Indeed, revivalist Calvin Colton (1789–1857) believed that it was *only* in America that the conditions were right for revivals; those conditions included "that mighty engine of human improvement—the press—as well as commercial and social intercourse that is open, and constant, and generous."[20]

Christian worship was seen to be an essential tool in these efforts toward this transformation of society and its members. Beginning in the mid-nineteenth century, famous revivalists such as Charles Grandison Finney, Lyman Beecher, and George B. Cheever developed increasingly precise measures for the conduct of Christian worship, and these measures were formalized and tested in a variety of settings. A wide range of revival manuals was published, until by the 1850s "the technique was so stabilized that there could be a revival without revivalists."[21] The connection between revival-style worship and the regeneration of individuals and communities was direct and unambiguous. One Methodist revival manual encourages its readers to think in quite mechanistic, cause-and-effect terms about the relationship:

> A revival is not a miracle. There is supernatural power present, but acting normally, within the lines of cause and effect. . . . The connection between the right use of means for a revival and a revival is as philosophically sure as between the right use of means to raise grain and a crop of grain. I believe, in fact, it is *more certain* and that there are fewer instances of failure. Probably the law connecting cause and effect is more undeviating in spiritual than in natural things, so there are fewer exceptions.[22]

Those conducting revival-style worship were encouraged to include "short poignant praying," personal testimonies, periods of sociability ("One good hearty handshake is of more value than two long prayers or three long exhortations to them to be faithful. Get them by the hand and show real fervent interest in their welfare."),[23] the use of the "anxious bench" for penitent sinners, instrumental music and repetitive, easily memorized choruses, and kneeling for prayer. These mechanisms, it was claimed, rightly applied and properly adjusted, would invariably result in a uniform "product": the revival of religion in individuals and communities. But always in these manuals there is the underlying message that what we have referred to as the "elimination of play" in the machinery of a revival was absolutely essential to its success.

Revivalism followed the machine-production model not only in its reliance on technique, but also in its entrepreneurial spirit. One author describes Dwight L. Moody (1837–1899) in decidedly commercial terms:

> His business was souls. And therefore he found himself confronting a market even more dazzling than an Imperialist of the countinghouse could conceive. For any product, no matter how cheap, there was a point of market saturation. But every human being on earth was a customer for salvation.[24]

For the later revivalists, salvation was a commodity to be "promoted," and worship was the principal "showroom" in which that commodity was marketed and sold (as well as the means of production by which that salvation was "manufactured.") And the promoters of salvation knew the importance of targeting a particular consumer market and designing the experience of worship so that it would "sell" salvation to the consumer. This approach, of course, presupposed an almost total commitment to liturgical pragmatism, the sense that whatever *worked* was necessarily right. Charles G. Finney spoke for most revivalists of the period when he defended the progressive development of his practical worship measures by arguing that "God has established, in no church, any particular *form*, or manner of worship, for promoting the interests of religion."[25] In a sense, the revivalists can be pictured as holding a Bible in one hand and a blank liturgical slate in the other.

Other religious movements also viewed Christian worship as a tool for the progressive improvement of the human product. The Social Gospel, with its radical blueprint for social reform rooted in a theology that stressed the historical reality of the kingdom of God, held that worship must be applied to the task of accelerating the advancement of the public conscience. At its height in the years just before World War I, able theologians such as Walter Rauschenbusch, Josiah Strong, and Washington Gladden produced influential sermons, books, and pamphlets setting out a vision in which services of public worship produced regenerated men and women who would redeem the moral order of society.[26] But there were to be other benefits as well, since the progressive development of religion (including worship), Christian ethics, and the American standard of living were bound up together. According to one Social Gospel proponent, Chester Carlton McCown:

> Progress *can* and *will* be made [in both religion and technology]. Electric light and power, the telegraph, the telephone, and the radio were impossible so long as men knew only the thunderbolt in the hands of Jupiter. [Improvements in] economics, ethics, and religion will catch up with technological improvements as soon as men learn to discard the superstitions and dogmatisms of the past and give themselves without reserve to the study of the facts of history, psychology, and society.[27]

Although the more pessimistic theological stance taken by theologians such as Reinhold Niebuhr (beginning with *Moral Man in Immoral Society* in 1932) had real influence, and disenchanted large numbers of Protestant liberals (as well as Roman Catholic and Jewish liberals), and some evangelicals, it probably failed to reach to the core of American religious optimism. Therefore, during most of the past two centuries, public worship in much of mainline Protestantism has been seen to be a part of the machinery of progress. And as worship itself progressed toward being perfectly suited to its task, as "play" was eliminated from the liturgical machinery, so too would Christian society progress toward perfection.[28]

COMPONENTIALITY AND EXPERTISE

Both the ideal of progressive perfectibility and the quest for the elimination of play in machines and production systems are dependent upon the concept of "componentiality," the idea that every system is made up of independent and self-contained units that, when brought into contact with other such units, form a working whole.[29] This model is applied not only to complex machines, but also to persons (as individual organisms or as elements within, for example, a social system or a labor force), and it can be contrasted to more organic models of organization and analysis. The scientific-management principles of Frederick W. Taylor have been mentioned earlier,[30] and it was Taylor, with his single-minded quest for the integration of workers into a machinelike system of production, who first applied the notion of component parts to the workplace:

> [Taylor] intended to do for the machine-worker interaction what nineteenth-century engineers had done for the interacting components of machines: to eliminate wasted motion, save energy, and rationalize functional relationships. The worker would become a component in a more encompassing mechanism, or system, for production. Taylor wrote . . . that in the past people had been first but, in the future, the system must be first.[31]

There is the strong tendency in this model to view all components as being of equal value, since each one in its right place is necessary to the proper functioning of the system.

The increasing fragmentation of the human experience of work that has resulted from the wide application of this model of production has been heavily commented upon by social analysts. In his comprehensive critique of industrialization, *Technics and Civilization*, Lewis Mumford looks at the ways in which human beings become "mechanized" and claims that as systems of manufacture broke down the process of production into a series of specialized operations, human beings became increasingly seen as component parts in the machinery of production. "Each one of these operations was carried on by a specialized worker whose facility was increased to the extent that his function was limited."[32] Although the dehumanizing effect of understanding men and women as component parts of a complex machine-production system has had ardent and articulate critics during the past one hundred years (Karl Marx said that mechanized manufacturing "transforms the worker into a cripple, a monster, by forcing him to develop some highly specialized dexterity at the cost of a world of productive impulses and faculties.")[33] the power of systems approach to the problems of production has been almost unassailable.

The "systems approach" to problem solving has transformed a number of the helping professions, from personnel management to family therapy, and it has had a certain degree of influence on congregational studies in the past twenty years. In this method, one seeks to understand a complex human system by isolating the individuals that are the component parts, analyzing their interaction (noting points of friction and improper alignment), and seeking to adjust the "machinery" of the various relationships and interrelationships so that the system operates more smoothly. As James Hopewell observes in his recent book on the nature of the congregation:

> The mechanistic examination of a potential dwelling uncovers how effectively the house fulfils its functions. . . . Such concerns about the efficiency of a dwelling also characterize a type of inquiry about congregations that came to national prominence as contextual approaches receded. New emphasis was placed in the internal operation of the local church, less stress was placed on its environment. Though aware of the social and cultural context of the church and the necessity of an evangelical engagement with it, advocates of the mechanist approach required that prior attention be given to the adequacy of the instrumentality that undertakes the engagement.[34]

In this model, worship is a component part in the congregational "system." To the extent that worship functions smoothly, it contributes to the effective functioning of the larger congregational "machine."[35]

There have been some very real advantages to the "systems approach" as it has been applied to certain areas of the practice of ministry. In various forms of pastoral counseling, for example, it has subverted the tendency to assign blame to individual members of a family or a congregation, and has helped both counselors and clients to see that each person's behavior can only be understood in relation to the behaviors of others in the system.[36] Recently, however, the ideological domination of "the system" has been quite heavily criticized. Philosopher Eugene Rochberg-Halton says that the system "represses the place of uncertainty in practice and the begetting of new problems and possibilities that are essential to all conduct from the most personal to the broadest institutional levels."[37] In other words, analysis of "the system" promises all the answers, and fails to allow for the natural interplay of divergent opinions and solutions, not to mention the intervention of what theologians would call "grace."

A direct result of both the quest for the elimination of play and componentiality is the increasing reliance on professional expertise. In a complex machine, it is necessary that there be someone responsible for the individual specifications of each component part, in order for that part to be precisely suited to its task so that the whole machine might run smoothly. And to the extent that the machine-paradigm is applied to a given human system or activity, there is a concomitant rise in the provision of suitable expertise to ensure *its* reliable functioning. Many have cited the relationship between the increasing influence of the machine-model of the human body and the expansion of specialized expertise in the medical profession as an example of this attitude,[38] but it is a clear trend in other professions as well.[39]

Increasingly, as the machine-paradigm has been applied to the Christian congregation and its activities, as well as to the individual and his or her religious life, ordained ministers have been expected to have the degree of professional expertise necessary to keep these running smoothly.[40] This has been expressed in both the fragmentation of academic theological disciplines and the expansion of ministerial specialties (e.g., hospital chaplaincy, recreation ministries, parish administration, religious education, liturgical or spiritual formation). Sociologist of religion Jackson Carroll links these trends to the rise of technological thinking, under the influence of which "It became important to the emerging professions to demonstrate that their practice was grounded in scientifically based theory that could be translated into skills for addressing important human problems."[41]

As the mechanical model has begun to be applied more specifically to the liturgical life of individuals and congregations, there has been a higher expectation that clergy will have professional expertise shaping and conducting Christian worship. Increasingly, as we have seen, seminary faculties of all denominations include academically well-qualified teachers of liturgy, who offer specialized courses in worship history, theology, and practice. In many cases, these courses themselves follow the machine paradigm, as they give sustained attention both to the various internal components of worship and to the ways in which worship operates as a component part in the larger systems of congregational life.

THE CONSEQUENCES OF MECHANISTIC THINKING FOR WORSHIPERS

One can begin to see from this that individuals who enter into the experience of Christian worship with this sort of package of consciousness will be making certain assumptions about the nature of that worship and their engagement with it. Participants may apply the ideal of incremental perfectibility to the rites, to the experience of worshiping, or to themselves as worshipers. They may view worship as a "product," which is designed and manufactured to meet their particular spiritual and religious needs. They may see the liturgy as a "system" in which they are a component part with a specific function, or as a complex machine that needs the intervention of experts in order to keep it running smoothly. Direct evidence for these views is difficult to come by, and largely anecdotal in character. But those who lead Christian worship are certainly aware of the force the machine paradigm exerts on individual worshipers and worshiping communities, and those who offer advice and training for the various kinds of pastoral-liturgical ministries usually take mechanistic attitudes for granted in their approach to liturgical questions.

In a number of popular manuals for clergy and lay worship leaders, the factory model as it was first envisioned by Frederick Taylor in 1911 is now applied (albeit unconsciously) to the local church, which is conceived as a modern workplace in which certain component parts of the liturgy, both ritual and human, are brought together, play is eliminated, and productivity increased. An extended quotation in one such manual will make the point. In their 1987 book *Leadership in a Successful Parish*, Thomas Sweetser and Carol Wisniewski Holden describe the debilitated state of congregational liturgy:

> Unfortunately . . . the worship life of many parishes leaves much to be desired. . . . No attempt is made to adapt liturgies to the needs of different groups, ages, or expectations. . . . Each group of liturgical ministers performs its job, working independently of others, following its own schedule and mode of operation. So much is lost in terms of creativity, initiative, and inspiration.[42]

The authors describe the solution to this condition of liturgical "friction" in terms that would make Frederick Taylor proud. What is needed is the ecclesiastical counterpart of scientific management!

> But gather these ministers together and . . . encourage them to brainstorm their ideas for improving the Masses to suit changing clientele, challenge them to perform their ministry better, link them together in a corporate effort at providing parishioners with a good occasion for worship, require from them periodic self-evaluation of their work, and the weekend liturgies will take on a new tone and character.[43]

Substitute the word *worker* for *minister*, substitute *product* for *Mass* or *worship*, and *factory* or *workplace* for *parish* and you see that this is a perfectly coherent Taylorist model for the efficient and productive manufacturing center. Play is eliminated by "linking" the workers in a "corporate effort," and a "new and improved" liturgical product is the result. Sweetser and Holden offer a plan for parish reorganization in which the entire workforce is to be redesigned to produce more efficiently the product best suited to the needs and desires of the consumer.

The seriousness with which these sorts of recommendations are taken has engendered a pervasive sense that we are all engaged in a continuous process of professionalized "tinkering" with Christian worship. Linked to this is the high expectation by participants that tinkering will result in increased emotional, psychological, and spiritual "satisfaction" from the liturgy. There is also an increasing tendency to withdraw commitment if that expectation is not met, to move to another congregation or denomination. According to Robert Wuthnow, "denominational switching" (the religious equivalent of "brand switching") is a significant factor in contemporary American religious experience:

In 1955, a Gallup poll showed that only 4 percent of the adult population—1 person in 25—no longer adhered to the faith of their childhood. Some 30 years later, another Gallup poll showed that 1 person in 3 had switched from the faith in which they had been raised.[44]

Wuthnow cites rising levels of education, intermarriage, and social and geographical mobility as the primary causes. But he also alludes to the fact that most religious people now have the experience of the worship life of denominations other than their own. In a 1984 survey, four out of five Americans had attended religious services in another denomination. Three out of five had attended worship in at least three different denominations, over half the population four or more different denominations, and one-third of the population sampled had attended services in five or more denominations.[45] With that kind of "liturgical supermarket" from which to choose, and with the sense of worship as a religious "commodity," the quest for satisfaction from the experience of worship must also be cited as a factor in denominational switching.

LITURGY AS TECHNOLOGY

To-day I think I have been edified and encouraged by reading two of dear William Penn's sermons, preached more than one hundred and fifty years ago. . . . One of the sermons was preached at a wedding when a Quaker wedding was a serious thing, a solemn religious institution. But now our excellent discipline is too much changed . . . and I fear is too much like the labor saving and money saving machinery of the day.[46]

What Quaker painter Edward Hicks perceived in the mid-1850s has developed in such a way that today, in various quarters, the liturgy itself has begun to be spoken of as a spiritual and religious "technology." Liturgist Roy Rappaport, for example, describes Christian worship as a "ritual mode of production," with the "product" an increasingly "numinous experience" in the worshiper.[47] He likens the action of liturgy to that of a printing press:

> As the press imprints an apparently invariant message on the paper passing through it, so a liturgical order imprints apparently invariant messages upon individual lives and upon society as a whole at intervals that it itself imposes on continuous duration.[48]

This sort of mechanical way of thinking about contemporary Christian worship also affects the way services are constructed (and, hence, experienced). In many cases, the worship leader or team will assemble various components from a variety of sources, and arrange them in such a way that they fit into a more complex liturgical structure. Historic rites "cannibalized" for parts to put into new liturgical bodies. Do-it-yourself packages of worship materials, abundant on the shelves of religious book shops, are meant to be culled and the pieces fitted together; some denominations have even taken a "loose-leaf-binder" approach to their authorized services.[49] The most recent example of the "machine-part" approach to liturgy is the computer software package "WorshipMaster," which offers instant access to thousands of individual liturgical components: hymns, visual material, prayers, litanies, creeds, and various other acts of worship.

This sort of technological approach to the building of liturgical systems means that there has been an additional need to eliminate as much friction as possible from the worship components. The parts must somehow be made to work smoothly, and the quality of resulting product must be predictable and (ideally) of uniform quality. The result has been what one seminary professor of liturgy calls "the new rubricism." Leonel Mitchell argues persuasively that "the breath of freedom and fresh air introduced by the revision of the liturgy is being quenched by the urge to get all the right choreography down on paper, so that we can all do it the same way."[50] As evidence, Mitchell cites the renewed popularity of liturgical manuals such as Howard Galley's *The Ceremonies of the Eucharist*,[51] and Byron Stuhlman's *The Prayer Book Rubrics Expanded*.[52] (Don Saliers' and C. D. Hackett's more recent *The Lord Be With You: A Handbook for Presiding in Christian Worship*[53] is another of this genre, the result of a coalition between the Methodist and Episcopal traditions.) It can certainly be argued that these books presuppose the kind of mechanical model of the liturgy we have been describing, a model in which each liturgical component can be isolated and each liturgical participant must have a clearly defined role and function in order for the liturgical "machine" to function properly. Galley, for example, segregates the liturgical function of each category of worship participant, whose activities are detailed in parallel columns so that the action might be fully coordinated.[54] This mechanized approach to participation in Christian worship also colors the interpretation of the historic rites that legitimize contemporary liturigical practice. Galley says in his preface, "The ceremonial of the fourth and immediately following centuries was essentially functional. The basic purpose was to underscore the meaning of what was being done or said. It also provided for the orderly participation of many liturgical functionaries."[55]

This kind of rereading of liturgical history through mechanistic spectacles is fortunately not common. But it does show the power of the machine paradigm to alter our perceptions, not only with regard to our present worship practice, but the practice of our Christian ancestors as well.

COUNTERMEASURES

There have been various important attempts to counteract the effects of machine thinking on worship and worshipers. The earliest liturgiological work in England and on the European continent was done in the context of the nineteenth-century Industrial Revolution, and much of this work can be described as an attempt to build liturgical fortresses against the dehumanizing and despiritualizing forces of industrialization and mechanization.[56] For many scholars working during this period, the study of Christian worship served the medieval ideal and aimed at accelerating the church's return to that "Golden Age," when it was believed that liturgy and life were fully integrated into an organic unity. Among Roman Catholics this expressed itself in attempts at the restoration of monasticism, and the recovery of monastic liturgical traditions; in Anglican circles the Cambridge and Oxford movements strove for a recreation of liturgical ornamentation and ceremony, of medieval buildings,[57] and of ecclesiastical and social organization.[58] Many Lutheran and Calvinist liturgiologists in this period were embarked upon their own romantic quests, but in these cases it was usually a romanticism about the Reformation period that was the driving force.

During this same period, those making historical-textual studies of the early liturgy deliberately chose organic models over mechanical models to explain the relationships and interrelationships between rites. Anton Baumstark (1872–1948), for example, appropriated the methodology of comparative anatomy, describing liturgy as developing under the same laws that govern other living organisms, with clearly definable "family trees" and lines of descent.[59] Only recently has this presupposition about the nature of liturgy been challenged.[60]

Early-twentieth-century Roman Catholic theology also bears the marks of the impact of industrial and mechanical models on religious life, and in various ways it too sought a more organic way of thinking about the church's liturgy. In the reintroduction of the "Mystical Body" motif in ecclesiology, the Roman Catholic liturgical movement found a stable foundation for a relationship between liturgy and life which, it was hoped, would curb the impact of mechanization. The worship of the Mystical Body was conceived as a corporate act wherein the whole Christ, head and members, unites to offer worship to God the Father. In the face of the deep fragmentation of industrialized society, active, intelligent, and faithful participation in Christian worship would result in a reintegrated and revivified community, transformed by individuals who could claim as their own St. Paul's dictum: "It is no longer I that live, it is Christ that lives in me" (Galatians 2:20).

The papal encyclical *Mystici Corporis*, promulgated by Pope Pius XII on June 29, 1943, set the seal on the direction the liturgical movement was taking by declaring that the Mystical Body was an appropriate model for the church and a proper source of theological and liturgical reflection. Later, this was superseded by an emphasis on incarnation as a liturgical and sacramental prototype,[61] and more recently has shifted to attempts to locate the church's worship within the framework of a theology of creation. But the influence of the older, mechanical models of sacramental and liturgical grace has remained quite strong, at least in the popular imagination.

CHAPTER
SEVEN

TECHNOLOGICAL RISK AND TECHNOLOGICAL COMPLACENCY

To the protected work
They fled, to the unsafe machinery
They lived by. "It will be better this time,
We have arranged, at last,
To succeed. Better luck
This time."[1]

We have seen how machine-paradigm thinking has shaped the consciousness of the Christian worshiper, and how the various aspects of that thinking—progressive perfectibility, componentiality, the elimination of "play"—have led to significant changes in the experience of participating in and reflecting on the liturgy. But there are two other aspects of the technologized worldview that have an equally profound effect on participants in Christian common prayer. Technological artifacts and processes are, in Merton's words, the "unsafe machinery we live by." They are the occasion for a high degree of risk, and they help to create in the late-twentieth century a globalized climate of risk.[2] But at the same time, technological artifacts and processes also help to create a climate of comfort, satisfaction, and safety, as they provide for various kinds of human needs and desires. Technology is both the cause of and the solution for the most pressing problems of the day, and the ambiguous relationship between these two seemingly opposite facts is a part of the "mental furniture" of the contemporary Christian worshiper.

Life has always been full of risk. Natural disasters, human violence, freak accidents, crop failure, and plague have been factors that have conditioned the consciousness of the Christian worshiper in every age. But there is something qualitatively different about risk in the contemporary technological age. First, we are aware that most technologies have what the Cambridge sociologist Anthony Giddens calls "eccentric consequences"—chemical additives to foods may cause genetic abnormalities; toxic waste and caustic pollutants may irreparably damage ecosystems; video display terminals may bring about miscarriages, hyperactivity, or cancers in those who use them regularly; atomic energy systems may contaminate people and landscapes with radiation. In addition, because technological structures and hardwares are highly complex, we are forced routinely to put our individual and collective fate into the hands of experts, who know about these intricate and dangerous technological systems, who engage in delicate risk-assessment operations, and who are expected to fine tune them to acceptable levels of safety. Heightening the sense of the riskiness of contemporary life is the fact that through the electronic media we have had graphic presentations of the consequences of technological malfunctions brought into our living rooms. Televised pictures of Bhopal, Three Mile Island, Chernobyl, and the Challenger Space Shuttle are engraved on our memory.

There is, moreover, the sense that the destructive possibilities of technology are not being controlled by religious or ethical values, or even by a more generalized concern for human life, but rather by the values of business, economics, and international power politics. In other words, we do not tend to limit technological initiatives because they might be harmful to the environment or because their ultimate human consequences are unacceptable or unknown. Instead, limits on technology are established because nontechnological solutions are cheaper, because the profit margin of a particular technological application is insufficient, or because the use of a certain hardware might result in a shift in the balance of power somewhere in the world. Most of these controlling systems are essentially neutral, abstract, and distant from the day-to-day lives of ordinary men and women. Global monetary policy, the equilibrium of the stock market, seasonal availability of commodities, and political instability all play a part in determining how (and when and where) technological solutions will be applied to human problems. There is also the fact that the more frightful the human consequences of a particular technological application, the less we are able to anticipate or experience those consequences, "for, if things 'go wrong,' it is already too late."[3] In other words, we cannot "dabble" in high-risk technology.

Social analysts identify several reactions to the necessary dependence on experts, on abstract systems, and on specialized risk assessments that characterize life in a technological age. An increased interest in self-help methods and natural remedies, an emphasis on "back-to-basics" political platforms, a proliferation of merchandise that evokes nostalgia, a rising demand for personal privacy and interpersonal intimacy, and an expansion of consumer choices all can be seen to arise from a growing sense that we can neither comprehend nor control many of the essential circumstances which determine our lives.[4] Since most of us are unable to participate in the abstract systems that define and guide these contemporary, high-consequence, technological risks, we attempt instead to apply a range of these more limited and personalized, "risk-management techniques."

Ironically, at the very same time that technology has created a climate of intensified risk, it has also created a climate of trust and satisfaction. Complex technological systems keep traffic from snarling, buildings from collapsing in earthquake zones, banks from losing our money, airplanes from crashing, and heart-attack patients from dying. Although some of its individual manifestations may still have the power to astonish us, generally we take technology for granted; as Peter Berger says, we look upon technology as "inevitable, as part and parcel of the 'nature of things.' "[5] A strong belief in the overall benevolence of technology, and in its ability to improve the quality of life, is attested in a 1979 Harris survey cited by sociologist of religion Robert Wuthnow. When asked what would make the greatest contribution to the supremacy of America in the next 25 years, 89 percent of respondents said "scientific research" and 73 percent said "technological genius."[6] In spite of technology's potential for damage to ecological, biogenetic, and human systems, *high tech* is still a word that has the power to sell everything from snow tires to mouthwash for the American consumer.

For many, technology's ability to increase human freedom and autonomy, to maximize choice, and to improve the quality of life gives it a quasi-religious status. In 1900, Henry Adams went daily to the Paris Exposition to pay homage to the dynamo on display, and his rhetorical question echoes throughout the succeeding decades: "Why shouldn't the dynamo be worthy of worship?"[7] Today, many things encourage a positive response to this kind of question. To cite just one example:

> The supply of food in present Western society has grown less precarious for most of us. God now seems much less significant to its supply, and food curiously responds to the nature and rules of a new provisioner: technology. We even call our foods according to the holy names of technology: TV dinners, fortified bread, instant breakfast.[8]

It is easy to see why technologies that embody and promote humane, democratic, laborsaving and lifesaving principles might be considered to be worthy of praise and thanksgiving. In addition, the "mysterious" quality of many technological systems, and the power of the scientific "high priesthood" that is in charge of manipulating the technical systems adds to the awe and reverence for technology. Much of the worship of technology takes place at what Gregor Goethals calls "the video altar." Twenty-four hours a day, the television displays the symbols and rituals of technology to the "faithful": images of machines, new and improved products of manufacturing for sale, the promise of a better life through technology, holy places where consumers may acquire a "technological fix."

There is some objective evidence for the claim that, in some ways, belief in technology has usurped traditional religious belief. In 1979, 73 percent of respondents to a Harris survey said technology would be the catalyst for national greatness; only 57 percent said "deep religious beliefs" would serve the same purpose. (This statistic led Wuthnow to describe faith in technology as faith in something "more objective than God.")[9] Whereas in the past things that were felt to be out of our control might have been handed over to the power of God, a certain segment of the population now hands those things over to the power of technology. Technology is aimed at satisfying human needs and wants, and it does this very well indeed.

The climates of both technological risk and technological satisfaction have also made an impact on various aspects of formal religious belief and behavior. Many social theorists (among them Durkheim, Marx, and Weber) believed that with the growth of technological institutions the practice of religion, including worship, would eventually disappear. But it seems that just the opposite has been true. In the past one hundred years there has been an increase in the variety of types of religious expression, and commitment to regular worship has remained relatively stable.[10] There has also been a creative reworking of certain central religious concepts in response to the challenges of technology. For example, Harry Emerson Fosdick, preaching just after the Second World War, interprets the nature of human sinfulness from under the shadow of the technologized horrors of Hiroshima and Nagasaki:

> The situation puts a fresh and serious meaning into the word "sin." . . . The old savage is no longer merely the old savage, but is now the primitive barbarian armed with the instruments of modern science. When one thinks of sin today that fact moves up into the center of the picture, no petty breaches of moral custom such as too often the church has wasted its time upon, but this huge matter, that something is abysmally wrong, an unredeemed savagery in the heart of man, can arm itself with the murderous instruments of modern science, and wreck the world.[11]

Some contemporary thinkers go so far as to say that the very possibility of a nuclear annihilation of human life disproves the existence of God altogether.[12] Alongside nuclear warfare, the experience of the Nazi Holocaust and the technology of genocide has led some theologians to undertake a serious reappraisal of traditional ways of talking about the omnipotence, omnipresence, and omnibenevolence of God.[13]

Although technology has allowed us to deepen and refresh our understanding of certain traditional religious concepts, many believe that it has at the same time made the development of genuine faith and insight more difficult. As we walk daily with technological risk, the sources of reliable and trustworthy authority are destabilized; as we transfer control over the time and place of apocalypse to the technocrats, the vision of an eschatological hope goes out of focus. On the other hand, technological satisfaction contributes to the sense that we are living in a world that is increasingly superficial, disposable, and ephemeral, that routinely turns luxuries into necessities, and that catapults us from one faddish imperative to the next without time for introspection.[14] This is the world out of which T. S. Eliot asks:

> Where is the Life we have lost in living?
> Where is the wisdom we have lost in knowledge?
> Where is the knowledge we have lost in information?[15]

For Eliot, as for many other observers of technological society, what is at stake is not religion or religious concepts, but our very humanity. The risk that technology may exterminate every form of life from the planet is real, but it is the power of technology to manufacture and then gratify our desires, and to anesthetize our pain, which will ultimately destroy us. We have found that we are able to use technology to manipulate nature, so that we can collectively and individually "avoid confrontation with the challenges of building a true community."[16] Before long, says Jacques Ellul:

> The edifice of the technical society will be completed. It will not be a universal concentration camp, for it will be guilty of no atrocity. It will not seem insane, for everything will be ordered, and the stains of human passion will be lost amid the chromium gleam. We shall have nothing more to lose, and nothing to win. . . . We shall be rewarded with everything our hearts ever desired. And the supreme luxury of the society of technical necessity will be to grant the bonus of useless revolt with an acquiescent smile.[17]

In the previous chapter, we saw the kinds of consequences that mechanistic thinking has for those who participate in Christian worship. Now we must ask, What particular challenges does the combination of technological risk and technological complacency present to liturgical prayer?

THE IMPACT OF TECHNOLOGIZED EVIL

Atomic, biological, and chemical warfare; technologized forms of genocide; and the exploitation and depletion of natural resources for profit—all are contributors to the creation of a world of technological risk. In various ways, the sense that sin and evil are more than simply (in Fosdick's words) "petty breaches of moral custom" has put tremendous strain on traditional structures of Christian worship. If technology has not changed the *quality* of human sinfulness and evil (and some would say it has indeed done exactly this), then it has at least extended its possible range, globalized its effects, and increased its potential for the annihilation of the planet.

One example will help to make the case. Many Jewish theologians and liturgists are beginning to come to terms with the exceedingly grave difficulties presented to traditional worship structures by the very fact that we now live in a world where Auschwitz-Birkenau and Bergen-Belsen are not only possible but also are generally *known* to be possible. The chemical technology that has made genocide available as a sociopolitical option and the media technology that has put that genocide into the public domain have forced many religious people either to abandon certain traditional elements of Jewish and Christian theology, or otherwise to reinterpret them so radically that faithful people living only a century or so ago would barely recognize them.[18] Although theologians continue to debate the question of whether or not the Holocaust was a unique event, or simply an unprecedented event, it is the very fact that the Final Solution was a *technological* solution which leads people to regard it as a definitive break in human history:

> The means without which this project could not have been carried out [are unique]. These include: a scholastically precise definition of the victims, juridical procedures, enlisting the finest minds of the legal profession, aimed at the total elimination of the victims' rights; a technical apparatus, including murder trains and gas chambers.[19]

For many Jews, the Holocaust has called into question such basic theological concepts as divine retribution, sin, providence, and the justice, mercy, and power of God, and it has shaken loose all of our old solutions to the problem of evil. For some, Elie Wiesel's chilling testimony of his experience in the camp strikes a responsive chord:

Never shall I forget those flames which consumed my faith forever.

Never shall I forget the nocturnal silence which deprived me, for all eternity, of the desire to live. Never shall I forget those mountains which murdered my God and my soul and turned my dreams into dust.[20]

For others, however, it is only in and through continuing faithfulness that the evil of the Final Solution will be redressed.

The "technology" of the camps also distorted certain more specific theological motifs. In his book *The Informed Heart*, Bruno Bettleheim (himself a camp survivor) tells of the ways in which the Nazis reduced their victims to machines by forcing them to perform meaningless work, and thus taking away their purpose in life. This had a direct effect on the theological substance of a central element in Jewish theology, the Sabbath, which is seen to be a cessation from one's work, and a dedication of that work to God. (This is the essential message of the Exodus story: freedom from slavery was freedom for *avodah*, service to God which is both worship and work.) When this work is coerced, purposeless, and dehumanizing, the offering itself is defiled.[21]

The difficulties for worship in this kind of situation are caused by the fact that certain forms of liturgical prayer, both Jewish and Christian, are founded upon a pre-Holocaust certainty about the sovereignty and mercy of God. For many Jewish theologians, the effect of the Holocaust on worship is seen to be analogous to the destruction of the Temple in 70 C.E. And just as it was then, the question today is, Where is God to be found now?[22] For Christians, there is a deep desire to worship a God who saves us not only from our own personal hard-heartedness and hatred, but also from the complex technological manifestations of hard-heartedness and hatred. Auschwitz stands as a roadblock to the realization of that goal.

Roman Catholic theologian David Power asks plaintively, "Can we in truth celebrate the eucharist after the Nazi Holocaust and in the face of imminent nuclear holocaust, and in a world half-populated by refugees, in the same way we did before the occurrence of such horrors?"[23] In other words, can we now confess and intercede before a God who seems not to have heard the cries of the Jews in the death camps? Do we want absolution from a God whom we have found guilty of indifference? Can we use the psalms which speak of the decisive intervention of God in situations of distress and injustice? Can we declare in the Lord's Supper that this is a God who has the power to save? Can we, in short, pray in the same way to the God of classical theism, the God of power, wisdom, might, and mercy, as a post-Auschwitz community of faith?[24]

Many Christians, of course, are indeed celebrating and praying in the same way. Some are convinced that in an age of heightened technological risk and technologized evil that Christian worship must remain steadfast and unchanging, a source of stability in a chaotic world. Some have retreated into individualism. Some have been unwilling to look into the faces of the six million for fear of losing their faith altogether, and can thus continue to worship as they have always done. But for many Christians, the technology of evil in the twentieth century has rendered most traditional forms of Christian common prayer both inaccessible and impotent. Theologian James Moore expresses the urgency of the current situation when he says, "it is the story, our story, that is threatened [by the Holocaust]. We are now challenged to see if we can tell our story still, without breaking, without admitting that it is a farce."[25]

MEDIA SATURATION

The importance of the pervasiveness of various forms of electronic media cannot be overestimated in any discussion of the intersection between technology and Christian worship. Media analyst Gregor Goethals describes television as the "video altar" at which vast segments of the American public worship every day. Just as the structures of Christian worship function as carriers of meaning in traditional religious contexts, the electronic media now function as bearers of meaning in technological contexts. The "tales of the good life" that Christian worship orders and proclaims are now rivaled by the "tales of the good life" on television and in advertising.[26]

From modestly designed ads in small newspapers to high-tech video commercials, advertising reaffirms the values we associate with the good life and reassures us that these are constant and obtainable.[27]

115

Clearly, the artifacts of technology are calling forth new forms of "faithfulness" ("I only buy SONY." "We swear by Ford cars."), and that faithfulness is encouraged, reinforced, and "sacramentalized" at the video altar. But it is not a simple case of large numbers of people swapping religious values for technological values, it is rather that there are increasingly diverse claimants to legitimate authority and thus to our allegiance. The media present us with a vast array of technological systems, institutions, individual specialists and experts, product and service advertisers, and religious and political leaders all seeking to exert influence over individual and communal choice. People cope in a number of ways with the dissonance caused by the varied and variable allegiances they are invited or expected to hold. They may succumb to the dominant authority, the authority that promises the most or speaks loudest or instills the greatest degree of anxiety about the consequences of refusing to comply. Or, like many young people in the 1960s, they may opt out of authority structures altogether. Most often, however, we tend to fall into patterns of commitment to a certain kind of lifestyle or routine that serves to organize our choices and our loyalties.

Both the lure of authoritarianism and the lure of routine have found their way into participants' expectations of Christian worship. We have already noted the multiplication and promotion of "authorized rites" in many of the mainline Protestant churches, which had previously been left with a high degree of freedom and autonomy. (The 1993 Presbyterian Church [USA] *Book of Common Worship* is the most recent example.) But another trend is even more significant as an indicator of how the shifting of traditional patterns of authority affect our expectations and demands of Christian worship.

Televangelism has managed to combine the need for stable authority, the devotion to technology, the desire for predictable and routinized worship patterns, and media commercialism into a multi-million dollar industry.[28] According to the 1991 Barna Survey, nearly half (48 percent) of all American Christians surveyed had watched religious broadcasting at least once during the previous year. (About a third of those surveyed had watched during the previous month.) For those who describe themselves as "born again Christians" the figure rises to 66 percent. During the decade between 1975 and 1985, Jerry Falwell, James Kennedy, Robert Schuller, Rex Humbard, and

Oral Roberts became household names, even for those who did not regularly watch their programs.[29] The worship conducted in and televised from their respective "megachurches" have several things in common: strong authoritarian leadership, a predictable (if not invariable) pattern, and promotion of religious commodities. Gregor Goethals finds a strong link between authority and merchandising and argues:

> As in ancient and medieval times, people today seem to depend upon some concrete, material expression which confirms and nurtures their sense of belonging—some tangible form of contact with authority and power. . . . Televangelists were quick to understand the importance of this sustained contact, and modern technology offers many new types of devotional forms—along with innumerable books, pamphlets, charts, and pins that are continually mailed out to loyal viewers. . . . Icons of tradition, their "magic" now sanitized and rationalized, have become acceptable forms of sacramentalism, sanctified by technology.[30]

In many cases, the authority of the leader is enhanced by "sidekicks" who defer to the leader's superior spiritual insight. The predictability of these services is also heightened by electronic subtitling or the display of the words of hymns and scripture readings on the screen. In many cases, the audience's need for routine and strong authority is also met by the theological framework of these worship services, in which there is a strong emphasis on the authority and sovereignty of God and on the development of a lifestyle that is governed by biblical principles.

Most of the people who regularly watch televangelistic worship services also attend services in church.[31] But the expectations of congregational Christian worship by those for whom televangelist worship is a steady diet has yet to be explored fully. (It is possible that two entirely different sets of expectations are operating within the worshiping community.) But those who are encouraging church growth, for example, seem to have derived their worship principles from televangelistic models of public prayer. They emphasize the providing of services of high technical quality that are predictable and easy to follow, with strong, clear liturgical leadership. If measurable church growth is the actual end result of these measures, perhaps this is some early indication of the transferal of the televangelistic paradigm to congregational worship.

One might think that the kind of discomfort with traditional prayer structures that we described earlier, and the quest for stability, predictability, and reliable sources of authority might be mutually exclusive. But they are tied together by a third trend in contemporary technological society: the high degree of dependence upon technology for the satisfying of short-term needs and a high degree of media investment in identifying and intensifying short-term needs. Advertising and the electronic media conspire to convince us that our physiological needs can be met by exercise gear and headache tablets, our psychological needs by tranquilizers and white-noise machines, and social needs by deodorants, silicone implants, and computer dating systems. For nearly every short-term problem there is a "technological fix." And because most persistent, long-term problems are *not* good candidates for simple technological solutions, they are routinely filtered out of the system and thus out of our consciousness.

This expectation that satisfaction will appear speedily in a technological package has a profound impact on Christian-worship participants, who are likely also to expect that spiritual needs will be met in a similar way—quickly, professionally, and without a high degree of personal effort required. For many people, congregational Christian worship becomes one more choice available in the spiritual supermarket. They are religious "consumers," with the power to choose congregational Christian worship over other forms of spiritual remedy, or to choose between competing forms of congregational Christian worship.[32] And both the available choices and the reasons for making a particular choice are now much more complex and diverse than they were even fifty years ago. For most participants, worship is judged by its ability to uplift, inspire, and console.

But its success at accomplishing those things is highly dependent upon its conformity to other elements of the technologized environment. As liturgist Frank Senn argues, "Those who have grown up with electric media are used to having their senses massaged and revitalized. Our culture itself has become highly sensate. Attendant to this has been a lower ability to concentrate on one medium for an extended period of time."[33]

Successful worship under these circumstances, Senn argues, is that which stimulates a number of senses at once, and uses a variety of different media of expression sequentially for brief periods of time. The popularity of slick, televised worship services broken up by sales pitches for religious products and services is only part of the reaction to this situation. There is some evidence that similar criteria are being applied to congregational worship services as well. For example, the performance of highly professional choral and instrumental music is often cited as an important factor in the maintenance and growth of churches, and quality music was given one of the most frequent responses in the 1991 Barna survey to the question, "Why do you go to church?" This is not only because people like the sound of good music, but also because it ensures a wider variety of kinds of sensory input. The contemporary worshiper is often most comfortable with fairly rapid "scene changes" from leader to choir to reader to instrumentalist to video display, with none of these demanding long periods of sustained attention.

CONCLUSION

While not all will agree with this description of congregational expectations of worship (the fact that the traditional sermon survives at all as a form of religious communication is the strongest argument against it), many clergy have recognized the trends and have accommodated their style of worship to them. On the whole, however, Christian worship has remained a fairly univalent, text-centered and, hence, word-centered experience. It continues to be an experience of the ear rather than of the eye, except to the extent that the eye follows on the printed page the words the ear is hearing. It seems likely that the gap between the technologized, media saturated, quick-fix world that most worshipers inhabit in their daily lives and the structures of traditional Christian worship, which demand deeper and more sustained attention and engagement, will continue to grow. How (or whether) the dissonance that this situation sets up will be resolved is difficult to predict.

Technological risk and complacency, crises of authority, and the expectations engendered by electronic media saturation are all likely to be with us well into the twenty-first century. And if people continue to consider Christian worship a spiritual, religious, or psychosocial necessity, they will continue also to bring these issues into the experience of Christian common prayer. A vast array of questions rise to the surface in the modern world, which Christianity and technology inhabit together. Can traditional structures of prayer withstand the pressures of technological risk? Can contemporary worshipers find ways of releasing the prayer that is within them through forms of Christian worship rooted in a pretechnological world? Can worship continue to claim authority as a source of religious nourishment and direction? But perhaps none of these questions can be answered without first addressing the larger issues: to what extent should Christian worship be created and understood as a countercultural force, an activity that calls into question the values and presuppositions of the age of technology, and to what extent it should conform to the kinds of contemporary expectations that the prevalence of technology has fostered? It is just possible the very survival of Christian worship as a form of religious expression depends upon the answer.

CHRISTIAN WORSHIP AND TECHNOLOGY IN DIALOGUE

So long as we are pilgrims in the world faith is implicit, not only as yet many things are hidden from us, but because involved in the mists of error, we attain not to all. The highest wisdom, even of him who has attained the greatest perfection, is to go forward, and endeavor in a calm and teachable spirit to make further progress. . . . God [gives] to each a measure of faith, that every teacher, however excellent, may still be disposed to learn.[1]

There has been a growing conviction in recent years that technology and its influence on society are unalterably opposed to the practice of religion, and particularly to Christian worship. Liturgy is perceived as being in a state of crisis and occupying a cultural ghetto, unrelated to the dominant culture that surrounds it.[2] As an expression of the faith of a deviant subculture, Christian worship may be engaged in the transformation of the world of technology or in the elimination of its effects, but it must never in any way capitulate to it. In addition, most people are convinced that this crisis is something relatively new, that certain forces peculiar to technologized modernity are responsible for the marginalization of Christian worship from the lived experience of contemporary men, women, and children.

As we have seen, this analysis is neither helpful nor accurate. This is not only because nearly every person who will participate in an act of Christian worship next Sunday morning will also be caught up in the experience of technologized living during the rest of the week, but also because technology and the liturgy have been involved in mutual interchange in every period of human history. In addition, the notion that Christian worship is unconditionally good and healthy and technology is unconditionally bad and unhealthy must also be challenged. As a part of their essential motivation, both Christian worship and technology have been elements in the quest for a better world, a world in which individuals can realize their true humanity and in which suffering, hunger, disease, and despair are pushed to the margins of human experience. Of course, both liturgy and technology have sometimes failed at this effort, since both also have the potential to numb the senses, deaden the conscience, and create climates of anxiety, injustice, and despair.

This book is based on the assumption that the mutual interaction between Christian worship and technology presents serious challenges to both these arenas of human experience. To the extent that worship can embody and sustain Christian love, hope, and charity then the dehumanizing, fragmenting, death-dealing elements of technology will be called into question. To the extent that technology can enhance the sense of human freedom, the unity of the global family, and the possibility of self-transcendence, then the irrelevant, individualist, and repressive elements of worship will be called into question. In other words, if technology and worship can enter into a relationship of mutual critique, there is the possibility that both may undergo genuine renewal.

But there are a number of constraints on this dialogue. For example, it is almost impossible, in these early days at least, for a discussion between worship and technology to be conducted completely in the abstract. We are very likely to be misled by speaking about "technology in general," since technology is not one thing, but an array of different things that have affected the world and its contents in a variety of different ways.[3] This is why I have focused individually on printing and clocks and bureaucracies and television and atomic bombs and other very specific manifestations of the technological impulse. At the same time, we are equally likely to be misled by speaking about "worship in general"—since, like technology, worship is also a constellation of different acts, images, and structures, meeting a variety of human religious needs. One of the things that has frustrated the establishment of a dialogue between worship and technology in the past is the reification of both technology and liturgy that tends to pervade the literatures of both disciplines.

We are left now to begin to ask how a useful dialogue between technology and technological structures on the one hand and liturgy and liturgical structures on the other should be undertaken. If we are to take seriously the implications of what we have said above, what should this kind of dialogue look like?

1. *It must include a wide variety of participants.* One of the things this study has shown is that technology affects and has affected Christian worship at a number of interpenetrating levels. Because of this, seminary professors, Christian worshipers, media analysts, church bureaucrats, mystics, working clergy, theologians, sociologists, and technology experts must all be engaged in this discussion, and must be engaged in it *together.* Bureaucrats need to hear from congregations and pastors how their work is being received. Clergy must tell seminary professors which elements of their preordination training in worship are useful in their pastoral-liturgical ministry. Theologians need to hear what those involved in the media, virtual reality, and interactive video games have to say about the kind of faithfulness they are seeking to engender; historians and philosophers of technology need to help liturgiologists tap into the riches of their discipline, and vice versa.

Because these different arenas of specialization and expertise have become so thoroughly compartmentalized and isolated from one another, exactly how and where this debate might be conducted is unclear. The various professional societies for the study of Christian worship (the most influential of which are the North American Academy of Liturgy and *Societas Liturgica*) tend to limit participation by imposing rigid membership qualifications based upon academic and professional criteria. The American Academy of Religion might inaugurate an interest group in this area, but again, the Academy tends to fragment into highly specialized subgroups and to discourage the participation of those outside the field of religious studies. Ironically given the kind of negative critique we have made of bureaucracy, it may be only a bureaucratic structure that could set up and manage such an ongoing dialogue. But at that point the process is immediately susceptible to all of the negative features of the bureaucracy itself—compartmentalization, the dominance of professionalized expertise, an inability to hear and respond to feedback, and a tendency to force the product into conformity with a preconceived shape and style.

2. *It must present a real challenge to technology.* As we have seen, technology has the power to further the highest human aspirations, to eliminate disease and hunger, to expand power bases, and to give individuals a sense of increased control over their own futures. But at the same time, as we have also seen, it has the power to increase superficiality, social fragmentation, and materialism, and to cause grievous harm to human and environmental health. In any dialogue between worship and technology, the participants must take the power of technology seriously.

But they must take the power of worship seriously as well. Christian worship has the power to shape individuals and communities; to provide a vision of the world as God intends it to be; to inculcate the biblical values of justice, peace, and the integrity of creation. We must try to restore the sense that was so important to the early pioneers of liturgical movement and the proponents of the Social Gospel that men and women and children, transformed by a deep engagement with the spirit of Christian common prayer, can in turn transform the society of which they are a part.

With this as a basis, the dialogue will be one that invites participants to find the precise ways in which Christian worship can identify and challenge the negative power of technology. Of course, beginnings have already been made here and there. For example in his essay "From Holy Meals to TV Dinners," James Hopewell argues:

> At a time when McDonald's is pushing its totally individualized "McFeast" concealed in a private package and consumable without reference to anyone else, a gospel ministry should renew the celebrative and communal aspects of feasts. Feasts, especially when the Eucharist is prominent within them, may be antidotes to lonely and godless eating.[4]

But unless the potency of Christian worship is taken seriously, these kinds of statements will lack any real conviction. We will be unable to see how the various elements of Christian worship—preaching and proclamation of Scripture, the initiation of new members, the proclamation of resurrection hope in the context of burial, the public declaration of God's willingness to forgive—have actual and specific implications for the decisions we make about the direction and use of various technologies.

3. *It must present real challenges to Christian worship.* While Christian worship may have the potential to transform the values of an age of technology, it has not often done so. As this study has demonstrated, in many cases worship structures and processes have supported the status quo, rather than contributing to social change. Those responsible for the worship life of congregations and denominations have not generally given careful attention to the ways in which certain kinds of technological values were influencing liturgical theory and practice. Both of these things need to be addressed within a wider discussion of the relationship between worship and culture.

In addition, there are important things we might learn from technology if we were to enter into a dialogue, in Calvin's words, with "a calm and teachable spirit." We have seen how technological systems succeed at expressing and nourishing certain values traditionally associated with religion, particularly faithfulness, commitment, trust, and a sense of possibility. Media specialists and product advertisers, for example, recognize the power of symbols and narratives to shape the human imagination and human identity, and they know how to create, out of words and images, the most potent, accessible, and enticing worlds in the public domain. Media-watcher Gregor Goethals is certain that Christian worship must learn from this ability to shape human aspirations if it is to survive: "Until institutional religion can excite the serious play of the soul and evoke the fullness of human passion, television will nurture our illusions of heroism and self-transcendence."[5]

What traditional liturgical images and symbols need to be abandoned as irrelevant to the lives of technologized people? What new images and symbols need to be adopted? And what are the principles that guide decisions in this area? In addition, as worship bureaucracies become more and more cumbersome, we need urgently to ask whether feeding the bureaucratic appetites of the system has begun to be more important than feeding the religious and ritual appetites of congregations and individual worshipers. Only a serious, ground-clearing discussion of the deep worship needs of Christians in the late-twentieth century can offer hope for renewal in this context.

4. *It must be broadly historical.* If we have learned anything from our brief case studies in the history of worship and technology, it is that there is not a single line of influence between one and the other, but rather that the two arenas of human experience intersect in various ways at various times. And because the church cannot know what it *can* do until it knows something about what it *has* done, a serious engagement between historians of the liturgy and historians of technology must lay the groundwork for future planning.

But liturgists also need to look more broadly at the place of history in their own discipline. Clearly, there are presuppositions that have been a part of classical liturgical studies about the place of historic rites and texts that may not be able to be sustained in a highly technologized society. Although a sense of the Christian tradition will continue to need to be nourished by liturgical structures, tradition will no longer be sufficient to *legitimate* those structures:

> With the advent of modernity. . . the routinization of daily life has no intrinsic connections with the past at all, save in so far as what "was done before" happens to coincide with what can be defended in a principled way in the light of incoming knowledge. To sanction a practice because it is traditional will not do; tradition can be justified, but only in light of knowledge which is not itself authenticated by tradition.[6]

This kind of situation invites us to reconsider how the history of Christian worship can become again a usable past for Christian worshipers.

5. *It must take theology seriously.* Those involved in the academic study of worship often complain that the other theological disciplines fail to take liturgy seriously as a valid source and expression of Christian belief. But the charge of isolationism can equally be laid at the feet of liturgists who, in restricting their discipline to a largely historical, text-based content, an analytical methodology, an excessive interest in primitivism, and a romanticism of the past have pushed the history, theology, and practice of Christian worship into an intellectual ghetto. Academic liturgists must begin to take more seriously the wider social, political, and economic world within

which Christian worship has functioned and continues to function if they are to keep their discipline from becoming increasingly marginalized. The study of technology in particular highlights how acute the challenge of contextualizing the discipline of liturgical studies has become. As we have seen, technology has intensified and accelerated the sense of religious and cultural dislocation in various ways. In a technological society all culture, including religious culture, is relativized. As Paul Ricoeur has said:

> When we discover that there are several cultures instead of just one and consequently at the same time acknowledge the end of a sort of cultural monopoly, be it illusory or real, we are threatened with the destruction of our own discovery. Suddenly it becomes possible that there are just *others,* that we ourselves are an "other" among others. All meaning and every goal has disappeared, it becomes possible to wander through civilization as if through vestiges and ruins. The whole of mankind becomes an imaginary museum: where shall we go this weekend—visit the Angkor ruins or take a stroll in the Tivoli of Copenhagen?[7]

Unfortunately, liturgical studies have too often been "a stroll through" East Syria in the fourth century, or Geneva in the sixteenth century, or Oxford in the nineteenth century. And both the intellectual isolationism and the intellectual compartmentalism of liturgical studies is contributing to, rather than challenging, the sense of dissonance and fragmentation. But if liturgists display a willingness to engage deeply with the spirit of a given age, including its technological spirit, they can make a real contribution to the reintegration of liturgy into the mainstream of religious life and thought.

The intersection between liturgy and technology opens up questions not only for the history, theology, and practice of Christian worship, but for other theological disciplines as well. What are the legitimate sources for ethical reflection and values clarification? How is a "prayed" Christology, or ecclesiology, or soteriology different from its academic counterpart, and how does it inspire people to action? How can God be said to be active in Christian worship and does this help us to comprehend God's activity in the world at large.

In the study of technology there may be a powerful model for contemporary theological reflection. In all areas of technology, there is a kind of provisionality about truth, a sense that nothing is certain except the immanent obsolescence of our certainties. As theologians we might very well, "take our cue from science, at once the source of our material achievements and the model of cumulative, self-perpetuating inquiry, which guarantees its continuation precisely by its willingness to submit every advance to the risk of supercession."[8]

6. *It must be genuinely pastoral.* In an age of technology, the challenges of building a true community, proclaiming and responding to the eschatological hope, restoring a genuine humanity, and coming to terms with sin, vulnerability, and death are particularly acute. We long to claim both our individual identity and our common humanity, and we seek a world in which power is used for dismantling barriers instead of erecting them. To forge a dialogue between Christian worship and technology that is truly pastoral is to forge a dialogue in a spirit of hope—hope for the future of worship, hope for the future of technology, hope for the future of the world.

But it is equally important that this hope be a genuinely Christian hope. This kind of hope:

> Does not demand a belief in progress. It demands a belief in justice; a conviction that the wicked will suffer, that wrongs will be made right, and that the underlying core of things will not be flouted with iniquity. Hope implies a deep-seated trust in life that appears absurd to those who lack it. It rests in confidence not so much in the future, but in the past.[9]

There are deep and well-founded concerns about the sociocultural instability that contemporary forms of the technological impulse are encouraging. But if Christian hope is indeed rooted in confidence about the past, it may be well to remember that the great ages of faith and renewal for Christian worship have been those that were most unstable: the third, sixth , twelfth, and sixteenth centuries. Renewal happens when people "break away from the dead hands and dead minds of the past, and are able to see and think creatively."[10]

But Christian hope must not delude itself. The practice of Christian worship in an age dominated by technology and technological thinking is in grave danger: in danger of becoming irrelevant and banal, in danger of becoming just another "technological fix," in danger of succumbing to the destructive values of technology, in danger of being locked into a religious or cultural ghetto, and yes, in danger of disappearing altogether. What is at stake here is not only the sanctification and redemption of individuals, but the sanctification and redemption of the world as a whole, including the world of technology. Technology can become sacramental, it can become a bearer of the self-giving love of God to a broken world. But in order for this to happen, Christian faith and practice must establish a genuine and ongoing discourse with technologized modernity. And students of Christian worship must be full participants in that enterprise. For in the experience of Christian worship we have the possibility of meeting a compelling God, who draws us into the future with assurance and forges us into communities bound by mutuality and sacrificial love. And in Christian worship we have the possibility of internalizing and making our own a vision of renewal and of the potential for holiness, which is intrinsic to every human person and every human structure. If Christian worship can speak to and within a world of technological hardware, processes, and presuppositions, then the search for God among the "nozzles and containers" may not be in vain.

NOTES

PREFACE

1. Throughout this book, although it runs contrary to much popular (and some academic) usage, I apply the terms *worship* and *liturgy* interchangeably to describe the phenomenon of public, corporate prayer.

2. Ian Barbour, *Ethics in an Age of Technology* (London: SCM, 1992).

3. Paul Bradshaw and Bryan Spinks, eds., *Liturgy in Dialogue* (London: SPCK, 1993), pp. 176-201.

1. RELIGION IN AN AGE OF TECHNOLOGY

1. David Jones, "A, a, a Domine Deus," which appeared in part in his *Epoch and Artist* (London: Faber and Faber, 1959), p. 179, and was first published in its entirety in *Agenda* 5:1-3 (1967), p. 5. Used by permission of the publisher, Faber and Faber Ltd.

2. From "The Scholar-Gipsy" (1853), stanza 21. Quoted from *The Poems of Matthew Arnold*, ed. K. Allott (London: Longman's, 1965).

3. On technology as "habitat," see Gayle Ormiston, ed., *From Artifact to Habitat: Studies in the Critical Engagement of Technology* (London: Associated University Presses, 1990). On technology as "environment" see "Technology as Environment" in Jacques Ellul, *The Technological Society* (New York: Knopf, 1964), pp. 34-50.

4. P. L. Berger, B. Berger, and H. Kellner, *The Homeless Mind* (New York: Vintage Books, 1973), p. 42.

5. Paul Tillich, *Systematic Theology, 3* (Chicago: University of Chicago Press, 1963), pp. 259-60. Others disagree with this analysis. Lewis Mumford, for example, says that it is not "manual work" but "cultural work" (art, literature, ritual) that is the distinctive mark of the human person. He does acknowledge that in previous ages manual and cultural work were practically and philosophically joined (*The Myth of the Machine* [New York: Harcourt, Brace and World, 1967], 102-4).

6. It is said that the term *homo faber* was coined by Benjamin Franklin. For Lewis Mumford's critique of the concept of *homo faber*, see his *The Myth of the Machine* (New York: Harcourt, Brace and World, 1967-70). See for the history of the interpretation

of technology Carl Mitcham, "Three Ways of Being with Technology," in Ormiston, *From Artifact to Habitat*, pp. 31-59.

7. Tillich, *Sytematic Theology, 3*, p. 73.

8. Ellul, *The Technological System* (New York: Continuum, 1980), p. iii.

9. There is the question of where the information technologies fit into this schema, and certainly some authors would suggest that information itself is a technological "artifact." See chap. 3.

10. See Ormiston, *From Artifact to Habitat*, p. 15 for a slightly different set of definitions, and also Stephen J. Kline, "Defining Technology," *Bulletin of Science, Technology and Society* 5:3 (1985), pp. 215-18. Both of these mainly are concerned with technological hardware. Social theorists Anthony Giddens, Jacques Ellul, Lewis Mumford, and Peter Berger all describe, in various ways, the shape of the technological "worldview."

11. See below, chap. 3, n. 47.

12. This engraving from Lyons and dated 1499 is a classic example of a *danse macabre*. For a reproduction, see Lewis Mumford, *Technics and Civilization*, (New York: Harcourt Brace Jovanovich, 1934), facing p. 76.

13. See Robert Alan Wauzzinski, *God and Gold: Protestant Evangelicalism and the Industrial Revolution, 1820–1914* (Rutherford, Penn., Fairleigh Dickinson University Press, 1993); John R. Griffin, *The Oxford Movement: 1833-1983: A Revision (Edinburgh: Pentland Press, 1984); Roger Aubert, Vatican I* (Paris: Editiones de L'orante, 1964); Torben Christensen, *The Origins and History of Christian Socialism, 1848-1854.* Acta Theologica Danica, 3. (Aarhus: Universitetsforlaget, 1962).

14. The popularization of the concept of postmodernity can be attributed to Jean-François Lyotard, *The Post-Modern Condition* (Minneapolis: University of Minnesota Press, 1985). Most recently the question of postmodernity has been explored by David Harvey, *The Condition of Post-Modernity* (London: Blackwell, 1989).

15. See Mumford, *The Myth of the Machine* (New York: Harcourt, Brace, Jovanovich, 1966), and *Technics and Civilization*, and Thomas P. Hughes, *American Genesis* (New York: Penguin, 1989).

16. Mumford, *Technics and Civilization*, p. 58.

17. Hughes, *American Genesis*, p. 330.

18. Quoted by Charles L. Stanford, "The Intellectual Origins of New Worldliness," in *Journal of Ecclesiastical History* 18 (1958), p. 16.

19. Hughes, *American Genesis*, p. 192.

20. Andrew Ure (1778-1857), "The Blessings of the Factory System" in *The Philosophy of Manufactures* (London: C. Knight, 1835), p. 22. Historian of technology Thomas P. Hughes describes the situation at the turn of the twentieth century: "By 1900 [America] had reached the promised land of the technological world, the world of the artifact. In so doing they had acquired traits that have become characteristically American. A nation of machine makers and system builders, they became imbued with a drive for order, system, control." Hughes, *American Genesis*, p. 192.

21. William Kuhns, *The Post-Industrial Prophets: Interpretations of Technology* (New York, Harper Collins, 1971), p. 137. See also David H. Hopper, *Technology, Theology, and the Idea of Progress* (Louisville, Westminster/John Knox Press, 1991).

22. The kind of mechanical precision that was applied to divine activity during the Enlightenment is exemplified by the work of French astronomer Pierre-Simon de Laplace who postulated the existence of a divine intelligence who, by knowing the velocities and the exact positions of all the atoms in the universe at any given moment, could determine both the history of the world and predict its future. See George Basalla, *The Evolution of Technology* (Cambridge: Cambridge University Press, 1988), p. 209.

23. See Lawrence J. Stone, *Crisis for the Aristocracy* (Oxford: Oxford University Press, 1965).

24. See especially for the history of the sense of self in society, Yi-Fu Tuan, *Segmented Worlds and Self: Group Life and Individual Consciousness* (Minneapolis: University of Minnesota Press, 1982).

25. See Ellul, *The Technological System*, pp. 10-17.

26. R. S. Thomas, from *Counterpoint* (Newcastle-upon-Tyne: Bloodaxe Books, 1990), p. 47. Used by permission of Bloodaxe Books Ltd.

27. Jürgen Moltmann, *The Theology of Hope* (New York: Harper & Row, 1967), p. 33.

28. See, for example, Ian Barbour, *Ethics in an Age of Technology* (London: SCM, 1992). Hans Jonas also takes this view, and suggests that an ethic suited to the global and long-term aspects of today's technology is largely lacking. See H. Jonas, *The Imperative of Responsibility* (Chicago: University of Chicago Press, 1984).

29. Francis Mannion, "Liturgy and the Present Crisis of Culture" in *Liturgy and Spirituality* (Collegeville, Minn.: Liturgical Press, 1990), p. 5.

30. Ibid.

31. George A. Lindbeck, *The Nature of Doctrine: Religion and Theology in a Post-Liberal Age* (Philadelphia, The Westminster Press, 1984), p. 22.

32. Anthony Giddens, *Sociology: A Brief but Critical Introduction*, 2nd ed. (London: Macmillan, 1986), pp. 15-16.

33. E. L. Trist, "The Structural Presence of the Post-Industrial Society" in F. E. Emery and E. L. Trist, *Towards a Social Ecology: Contextual Application of the Future in the Present* (New York: Plenum Press, 1972), p. 265.

34. Jacques Ellul, *The Technological Society*, trans. J. Wilkinson (New York: Knopf, 1964).

35. Jacques Ellul, *The Technological System*, trans. J. Neugroschel (New York: Continuum, 1980).

36. Jacques Ellul, *The Technological Bluff*, trans. J. Bromiley (Grand Rapids: Eerdmans, 1990).

37. Paul Tillich especially draws attention to this aspect of technology in "The Person in a Technological Society" in *Social Ethics*, ed. Gibson Winter (New York, Harper & Row, 1968).

38. Christopher Lasch, *The True and Only Heaven* (New York: W. W. Norton, 1991), p. 71.

39. See Barbour, *Ethics in an Age of Technology*.

40. Ibid., p. 24.

41. For manufacturing see Mumford, *Technics and Civilization* (New York: Harcourt Brace Jovanovich, 1934), for information technology see below, pp. 138-55, for biotechnics see Ian Barbour, *Ethics in an Age of Technology*, for media

see J. Meyrowitz, *No Sense of Place* (New York: Oxford University Press, 1985) and Harvey, *The Condition of Post-Modernity*, chapters 14-16.

2. TECHNOLOGY AS A CHALLENGE FOR THE STUDY OF CHRISTIAN WORSHIP

1. Ian Barbour, *Ethics in an Age of Technology* (London: SCM, 1992) especially part 2, pp. 85-178. Barbour highlights such things as the environment, nuclear technology, genetic engineering, agriculture, and information technology as being areas of special concern to contemporary ethicists and pastoral theologians. See also Gary R. Collins, ed., *Innovative Approaches to Counselling* (Waco, Tex.: Word, 1986), chap. 6, "Environmental Counselling."

2. This highly compartmentalized outlook mainly affects those at the far edges of what James F. White and others have termed the "liturgical right" and the "liturgical left"—the Orthodox, Anglican, and Roman Catholic traditionalist groups on the right; and the more evangelical segments of various denominations on the left. See J. F. White, *Protestant Worship: Traditions in Transition* (Louisville: Westminster/John Knox, 1989).

3. Liturgy as an academic discipline dates back to the mid-nineteenth century. Although the term *liturgics* is known as early as 1855 (John Ogilve's Supplement of that year to his *The Imperial Dictionary, English, Technological, and Scientific* defines *liturgics* as "the doctrine or theory of liturgies"), by 1882 both Philip Schaff (in the *Encyclopaedia of Religious Knowledge*) and William Blakie (*The Ministry of the Word*) can use it without further explanation. Slightly earlier is J. M. Neale, *Essays in Liturgiology* (London, 1863). Each of these presupposes that the study of liturgy is a distinctive and definable enterprise.

4. See, for example, Paul Bradshaw, *The Search for the Origins of Christian Worship* (London: SPCK, 1992), and B. Spinks, *The Sanctus in the Eucharistic Prayer* (Cambridge: Cambridge University Press, 1991). Thomas Talley has spent much of his long and distinguished career as a liturgist searching for the origins of the liturgical calendar, and the title of his book *The Origins of the Liturgical Year* (New York: Pueblo, 1986) testifies to this quest for liturgical roots.

5. William Crockett, *Eucharist: Symbol of Transformation* (New York: Pueblo, 1989), p. 230. See also Howard E. Galley, *Ceremonies of the Eucharist* (Cambridge, Mass.: Cowley, 1989), who says of the work on ancient texts and practices that, "It became plain to all involved that many of the older ways helped to elucidate the meaning of the liturgy in ways that later practices did not," p. xv.

6. Ibid., p. 231. See also Frank Senn, *New Eucharistic Prayers: An Ecumenical Study of Their Development and Structure* (New York: Paulist Press, 1987).

7. Bradshaw, *The Search for the Origins of Christian Worship*, p. 101.

8. Ibid., 110.

9. As we shall see, this way of dealing with texts is itself a product of technology, a sense that the text can be an interchangeable part. See below, chap. 3.

10. Psychology, sociology, and human biology have made important contributions to the study of Christian worship, see especially "What Biogeneticists Are Saying about Ritual: A Report" in *Liturgy Digest*, 1:1, pp. 39-68.

11. See for example, Victor Turner, *The Ritual Process: Structure and Anti-Structure* (Ithaca, N.Y.: Cornell University Press, 1982); Claude Lévi-Strauss, *The Savage Mind*, trans. G. Weidenfield (Chicago: University of Chicago, 1968); Mary Douglas, *Purity and Danger* (London: Routledge and Kegan Paul, 1966), and *Natural Symbols: Explanations in Cosmology*, 2nd ed. (London: Barrie and Jenkins, 1973); A. van Gennep, *The Rites of Passage* (originally *Rites de Passáge*) trans. M. B. Visedom and G. L. Caffee (Chicago: University of Chicago Press, 1960). The work by van Gennep has been particularly influential in the reform of Christian initiation rites.

12. Each of the authors cited in note 11 founded their research on tribal religions, Turner with the Ndembu in northwestern Zambia, van Gennep cited examples from various African tribal religions, and Douglas from the Dinka in Sudan and the Cheyenne of the Western Plains.

13. Frank Senn, *Christian Worship and Its Cultural Setting* (Philadelphia: Fortress, 1983), p. 10.

14. Emphasis added. See, for example, Victor Turner, *The Forest of Symbols* (Ithaca, N.Y.: Cornell University Press, 1967), p. 19; *From Ritual to Theatre* (New York: Performing Arts Journal Publications, 1982), p. 79; and Victor Turner and Edith Turner, *Image and Pilgrimage* (New York: Columbia University Press, 1978), p. 243. Ritologist Ronald Grimes has been particularly rigorous in pointing out the flaws in Turner's definition. In *Beginnings in Ritual Studies* (Washington, D.C.: University Press of America, 1982), p. 54, he states that "magical rites are occasions that refer to mystical powers in a technological manner and must not be definitionally separated from technology" and also that "technological routine itself has a ritual quality which ought not be overlooked simply because it does not refer to divine beings."

15. Turner, *From Ritual to Theatre*, p. 35.

16. Mary Douglas, however, is among the very few ritologists that see "secularism" at work universally and finds the same kind of fragmentation of experience (and the concomitant difficulty in the ability to ritualize) both in industrial societies and in the tribal societies on which she based her work. See *Natural Symbols* (New York: Pantheon, 1973), preface. Ernst Gellner is especially critical of the tendency to idealize the primitive, see his chapter in Brian Wilson, ed., *Rationality* (Oxford: Blackwell, 1977). Some scholars with interest in Christian worship, and particularly sacramental theologians, have tried to resist the effects of primitivism on the popular view of worship. In his 1980 book *From Magic to Metaphor: A Validation of the Christian Sacraments* (New York: Paulist, 1980), George Worgul identifies an attitude among observers of Christianity that "identifies Christian ritual as magical rites. In this instance, Christian sacraments are reduced to 'dated', 'primitive', and 'archaic' behaviors belonging to a previous era of humankind's history, . . . [which] portrays Christian ritual as an attempt to escape from 'real' post-industrial life," p. 223.

17. Also called *contextualization, acculturation,* and *indigenization.*

18. See S. J. White, *Art, Architecture, and Liturgical Reform* (New York: Pueblo, 1990), pp. 142-47 and *passim*.

19. *Constitution on the Sacred Liturgy*, III:37.

20. Ibid., III:38.

21. See for inculturation in the Roman Catholic tradition, Ansgar Chapungo, *Liturgical Inculturation* (Collegeville, Minn.: Pueblo, 1992). For inculturation in the Anglican Communion, see David R. Holeton, ed., *Liturgical Inculturation in the Anglican Communion, including the York Statement "Down to Earth Worship,"* Alcuin/GROW Liturgical Study 15 (Bramcotte, Notts: Grove Books, 1990). Also see George Minamiki, *The Chinese Rites Controversy: From Its Beginning to Modern Times* (Chicago: Loyola University Press, 1985).

22. See S. J. White, *Art, Architecture, and Liturgical Reform*.

23. See, for example, Ans J. van der Bent, *Vital Ecumenical Concerns: Sixteen Documentary Essays* (Geneva: World Council of Churches, 1986), especially chap. 9 "Worship and Spirituality," pp. 175-91.

24. Vincent J. Donovan, *Christianity Rediscovered* (Maryknoll, N.Y.: Orbis, 1982).

25. David J. Bosch, *Transforming Mission: Paradigm Shifts in Theology of Mission* (Maryknoll, N.Y.: Orbis, 1992), especially pp. 447-55.

26. Donald Gray, "Liturgy and Society," in *The Identity of Anglican Worship* (London: SPCK, 1990), p. 136. One might also cite Herbert Brokering's reworking of the Benedicite, "Earth and all Stars," commissioned for the ninetieth anniversary of St. Olaf [Minn.] College); *Lutheran Book of Worship*, no. 558; *Lutheran Worship*, no. 438; The Episcopal Church (USA) *Hymnal, 1982*, no. 412; and Brian Wren's "Praise God for the Harvest" which speaks of "The long hours of labor, the skills of a team/The patience of science, the power of machine."

27. These words from the poem of William Blake (1757–1827) have always been the battle cry of those warring against industrialization. The poem is used as one of England's best-loved national hymns, and set to the tune also titled JERUSALEM. Contemporary Blake scholarship suggests, however, that his reference to "dark satanic mills" here is to the church rather than to industry.

28. Daniel Bell, "Notes on the Post-Industrial Society" in *The Public Interest* part 6 (Winter, 1967), p. 62.

29. See H. Saint-Simon, *Nouveau Christianisme* (Paris, 1825).

30. Bell, "Notes on the Post-Industrial Society," p. 65.

31. This echoes Max Weber's view that through the bureaucratization of so many aspects of life we have lost the "personal and mystical" elements of our humanity. The question continues to be posed in philosophical discussions of the role of technology. As Daniel Yankelovich puts it: "Can we be fully human in a society dominated by technology and impersonal institutions?" His answer is a qualified yes. See his "Two Truths: The View from the Social Sciences," in Borchert and Stewart, *Being Human in a Technological Age*, pp. 89-105. See also the title essay in Martin Heidegger, *The Question Concerning Technology and Other Essays* (New York: Harper & Row, 1977), pp. 3-35.

32. Berger, *The Homeless Mind* (New York: Vintage Books, 1973), p. 133.

33. See chap. 1, p. 16.

34. See as an example of this kind of approach, Wayne Meeks, *The First Urban Christians* (New Haven: Yale University Press, 1983).

35. See Ovitt, *The Restoration of Perfection,* chap. 5. "The issue of manual labor was the first source of difficulty for the Cistercians, for they quickly discovered what earlier Benedictines had learned, that economic self-sufficiency was incompatible with the performance of the Divine Office" (p. 144). Lynn White, in *Medieval Religion and Technology* (Berkeley: University of California Press, 1978), is principally concerned with classical Benedictine monasticism, while Ovitt is analyzing various monastic rules, with special attention to the twelfth-century Cistercians. Although they adopt slightly different stances on the intellectual grounding of technology, both White and Ovitt trace the roots of several modern technological trends to the interplay of *ora* and *labora* in the Middle Ages.

36. See especially Frederick Sommers West, "Anton Baumstark's Comparative Liturgy in Intellectual Context" (unpublished Ph.D. Dissertation, University of Notre Dame, 1988).

37. Christel Lane, *The Rites of Rulers: Ritual in Industrial Society—The Soviet Case* (Cambridge: Cambridge University Press, 1981). It is interesting that Lane describes the initiation into a collective in almost the same terms as Turner describes the initiation into adult tribal society. "The initiation ritual is designed to mark an important transition in the life of a young person, to link him to a new collective and to provide him with new goals and ideals" (p. 112).

38. *Ritual in Industrial Society: A Sociological Analysis of Ritualism in Modern England* (London: George Allen and Unwin,1974). Unfortunately, Bocock relies on a limited number of social analysts (mainly Durkheim and Marx) and leaves unanswered the question of what a technological society *is,* and how its artifacts and processes actually relate to the liturgy.

39. See Ian Ramage, *Battle for the Free Mind* (London: George Allen and Unwin, 1967) especially chap. 10, "Charisma and Community." and R. F. Wearmouth, *Methodism and the Common People of the Eighteenth Century* (London: Epworth, 1985).

3. SHAPING WORSHIP IN THE TECHNOLOGICAL MODE

1. Mark Searle, "Private Religion, Individualistic Society, and Common Worship" in *Liturgy and Spirituality,* ed. Eleanor Bernstein (Collegeville, Minn., Liturgical Press, 1990), p. 27.

2. See, for a history of information technology, S. Saxby, *The Age of Information: The Past Development and the Future Significance of Computing and Communications* (New York: Macmillan, 1990).

3. M. McLuhan, *Understanding Media: The Extensions of Man* (New York: McGraw Hill, 1965), p. 20.

4. See F. A. Gasquet and E. Bishop, *Edward VI and the Book of Common Prayer* (London: Hodges, 1890), chap. 7.

5. *1 Apologia, 65*, Library of Christian Classics, vol. 1, trans. and ed. Cyril Richardson (Philadelphia: Westminster, 1953).

6. *1 Apologia, 67.*

7. See, for example, P. Maranus, in *Patrologia Graeca* (ed. Migne) 6, 429-30, and notes 89-90 and J. Kaye, *The First Apology of Justin Martyr* (Edinburgh, 1912), and J. Beran, "*Quo sensu intellegenda sint verba Sancti Justini Martyris hose dunamis auto in 1 Apologia, n. 67,*" in *Divus Thomas* 39 (1936), pp. 46-55.

8. See most recently P. F. Bradshaw, *The Search for the Origins of Christian Worship* (London: SPCK, 1992), pp. 159-60.

9. For the kind of caution which must be applied to the date, authorship, and place of this document in liturgical history see P. Bradshaw, *The Search for the Origins of Christian Worship*, pp. 89-92.

10. *Apostolic Tradition,* 9. For a critical text of the *Apostolic Tradition,* see Gregory Dix, *The Treatise on the Apostolic Tradition of St. Hippolytus,* 2nd ed. (London, 1937, 2nd edition, 1968). For a more accessible text, see G. Cuming, ed., *The Apostolic Tradition of Hippolytus: A Text for Students,* Grove Liturgical Studies, 8 (Bramcote, Notts: Grove Books, 1976).

11. See Allan Bouley, *From Freedom to Formula: The Evolution of the Eucharistic Prayer from Oral Improvisation to Written Texts,* CUA Studies in Christian Antiquity 21 (Washington, D.C.: Catholic University of America Press, 1981) for a systematic summary of this evidence.

12. This phrase is from Origen (*Conv. with Herac.* 4 in *Sources Chrétiennes* 67, pp. 62-64) who advises bishops "If it seems good to you, let these conventions *(sunthekais)* be in force." The "conventions" to which Origen is referring here are those that regulate that the prayer of the Eucharist be made through the Son to the Father. A pupil of Origen, Dionysius, Bishop of Alexandria, speaks of having "of course received a model and rule from the presbyters before us, [and] close our making of the eucharist in harmony with them: . . . To God the Father and to the Son our Lord Jesus Christ, with the Holy Spirit, glory and power for ever and ever. Amen." Cited in Bouley, *From Freedom to Formula,* p. 142.

13. *Apostolic Tradition,* 9. "If indeed anyone is able to pray suitably with a solemn prayer, that is good. However, if anyone when he prays recites a shorter prayer, do not prevent him. Only let his prayer be soundly orthodox."

14. See George A. Kennedy's two important books on this question, *Christianity and the Rhetoric of Empire: The Development of Christian Discourse* (Berkeley: University of California Press, 1991) and *Greek Rhetoric Under Christian Emperors* (Princeton: Princeton University Press, 1983). In his *Rhetoric,* Aristotle describes three kinds of rhetorical structure: the "juridical," which tries to presuade hearers to make a decision; the "deliberative," which is aimed at driving hearers to future action; and the "epideitic," which is structured to persuade hearers to hold or reaffirm some belief or opinion. *Rhetoric,* 3.1.1358a.

15. Bouley, *From Freedom to Formula,* says "At the end of the sixth century Rome has a Latin eucharistic canon, textually fixed except for a few later refinements. . . . Of oral improvisation there is no trace at all" (p. 201). But legitimate local variations continued to exist, even though they now tended to be encapsulated in written texts.

16. Several church councils were held at Milevis in the early years of the fifth century. The Council of Milevis referred to here was a local synod for the Numidian province of North Africa, at which Augustine was present as a bishop of that

province. The Council was particularly concerned with standing against Donatism. See the synodical letters in Augustine, *Epistolarum Classis III*, in J. Migne, *Patrologia* (Paris, 1845), pp. 758-60. It is not to be confused with the VII Council of Carthage, which met for one of its sessions at Milevis in 402 or with the Council of Milevis, which condemned Pelagius and Caelestius in 416.

17. Cited in Geoffrey Wainwright, *Doxology: The Praise of God in Worship, Doctrine and Life* (New York: Oxford University Press, 1981), p. 255.

18. It is always worth keeping in mind that the very term *orthodox* is in essence a liturgical term, implying rightness in praising God rather than rightness in thinking about God.

19. See Bouley, *From Freedom to Formula*, pp. 200-215.

20. Bouley suggests this when he says, "Oral improvisation certainly disappears and written improvisation goes into sharp decline after the sixth century, probably as a result of the Gregorian reforms *and because of the compilation and diffusion of text collections in the sixth and seventh centuries.*" (emphasis added), p. 211. But he fails to follow through on this point, and the scriptoria are not referred to in his book at all.

21. We see here as elsewhere in this period a true overlapping of oral and written cultures. Toward the end of this period, something of a division of labor arose in the scriptoria, with different groups of scribes working on different portions of a given manuscript. See K. W. Humphreys, *The Book Provisions of the Medieval Friars, 1215-1400* (Amsterdam, 1964).

22. Elizabeth Eisenstein, *The Printing Press as an Agent of Change*, vol. 1 (Cambridge: University Press, 1980), p. 16. This is by far the most penetrating and complete study of the history of printing available.

23. "The term *edition* comes close to being an anachronism when applied to copies of a manuscript book." Eisenstein, *The Printing Press as an Agent of Change*, p. 11.

24. See Bradshaw, *The Search for the Origins of Christian Worship*, pp. 73-74.

25. We know from extant manuscripts that in Bologna, for example, in 1280 paper was already six times cheaper than parchment.

26. Myron Gilmore, *The World of Humanism, 1453–1517*, Rise of Modern Europe Series, ed. W. Langer (New York: Greenwood, 1952), p. 186. See also Denys Hay, *Printing and the Mind of Man* (London: Cassell, 1967): "It is impossible to exaggerate the rapidity of the transformation," p. xxii.

27. The first dateable piece of work from Gutenberg's press was an indulgence.

28. To appreciate the scale of the work being done, note that one Barcelona printer, Johann Luschner, printed an order of 18,000 letters of indulgence for the Abbey of Montserrat in May 1498. See S. H. Steinberg, *Five Hundred Years of Printing* (Harmondsworth, U.K.: Pelican, 1955), p. 139. In Nuremberg at about the same time there was one large printing company "with 24 presses and over 100 employees—typesetters, printers, correctors, binders." Mumford, *Technics and Civilization*, p. 136.

29. We often say, "Necessity is the mother of invention," but in the case of the relationship between printing and literacy it seems to be the other way around. Printing created for itself a new market and increased literacy almost overnight. See Eisenstein, *The Printing Press as an Agent of Change*, pp. 27-33, 60-65 and Tessa Watt,

Cheap Print and Popular Piety, 1550–1640 (Cambridge, Cambridge University Press, 1991).

30. This from a treatise by Abbot Trithemius of Sponheim *In Praise of Scribes*. He also predicts that manuscripts on parchment will last longer than those on paper. See Eisenstein, *The Printing Press as an Agent of Change*, pp. 14-15. For the best edition of this work see Klaus Arnold, ed., *In Praise of Scribes—De Laude Scriptorum*, trans. R. Beherendt (Lawrence, Kansas: Universty of Kansas Press, 1974), pp. 24-26.

31. See Curt Bühler, *The Fifteenth-Century Book: The Scribes, the Printers, the Decorators* (Philadelphia: University of Pennsylvania Press, 1960), p. 16.

32. As did, of course, the sellers of other printed material, such as Johann Tetzel, whose sale of indulgences so outraged Luther.

33. Eisenstein, *The Printing Press as an Agent of Change*, p. 346, n. 148. From the invention of the press to 1520, 156 Latin versions of the Bible were published and 17 different German translations. The first French Bible was printed quite late, in 1523. Papal edicts from 1520 onward sought to curtail vernacular Bible production, and the first Index of Banned Books in 1564 prohibited both Bible reading and the printing of any version of the Bible other than the authorized Vulgate. This prohibition was repeated in all later editions of the Index. As we saw above, there was also a more general anxiety about the power of the printing press, which is expressed in the earliest known depiction of the printing press from Lyons, 1499, in which skeletons impede the workers at their work.

34. See Eamon Duffy, *Stripping the Altars: Traditional Religion in England 1400–1580* (New Haven, Conn.: Yale University Press, 1992); and for England see Watt, *Cheap Print and Popular Piety*, pp. 1-8.

35. *Actes and Monuments of Matters Most Speciall and Most Memorable, Happening in the Church . . .* , III (London: The Company of Stationers, 1595), p. 720. Foxe was a fervent believer in the revolutionary promise of the press. In his preface to a collection of Protestant texts (1572) he writes, "The excellent arte of printing most happily late found out . . . to the singular benefit of Christe's Church . . . will restore the lost light of knowledge to these blinde times."

36. This included not only indulgences, but lay missals, devotional manuals, expositions of the articles of faith, and books of moral instruction.

37. Mumford, *The Myth of the Machine*, p. 273.

38. "The printed book made all knowledge progressively available to all those who learned to read even if poor: and one of the results of this democratization was that knowledge itself, as contrasted with legend, dogmatic tradition, or poetic fantasy, became a subject of intense independent interest, spreading by means of the printed book into every department of life, and immensely increasing the number of minds, past, present, and future, having intercourse with each other." Mumford, *The Myth of the Machine*, p. 285. In 1543, a Papal decree forbade Bible reading to "women, artificers, apprentices, journeymen, yeomen, husbandmen, and laborers." See Eisenstein, *The Printing Press as an Agent of Change*, p. 358.

39. Mumford, *The Myth of the Machine*, p. 285. Luther called the printing press "God's highest act of grace."

40. As an important symbol of this, a final rubric in the 1549 *Book of Common Prayer* stipulates that of Edward VI "streightly chargeth and commandeth, that no manner of person do sell present booke unbounde, above the price of ii Shyllynigs the piece. And the same bounde in paste or in boardes, not aboue the price of three shyllings and fourepence the piece."

41. See James F. White, *Protestant Worship: Traditions in Transition*. Here White identifies nine discrete liturgical families. Printing also contributed to the solidification of linguistic and national boundaries as well as religious ones.

42. Eisenstein, *The Printing Press as an Agent of Change*, p. 355.

43. See, for example, Finklestein, *Windows on a New World: The Third Industrial Revolution* (New York: Greenwood, 1989). Also on the impact of networking, see "Wired" in *Newsweek*, September 6, 1993.

44. Thomas L. McPhail calls the globalization of computer networks and communications networks "electronic colonialism" and warns that "the dependency relationship established by the importation of communications hardware, foreign-produced software, along with engineers, technicians and related information protocols, that vicariously establish a set of foreign norms, values and expectations which, in varying degrees, may alter the domestic cultures and socialization processes. . . . Electronic colonialism of the twentieth century is just as dreaded as mercantile colonialism of the eighteenth and nineteenth centuries." in *Electronic Colonialism: The Future of International Broadcasting and Communications*, 2nd ed. (Sage Publications, 1987), pp. 53-54.

45. It is called *Leitourgia*, and has been developed by the Notre Dame Center for Pastoral Liturgy, Notre Dame, Indiana.

46. "Technology Review" in *Liturgy Digest* 1:1 (Spring, 1993), p. 149.

47. Certainly liturgists of the past did rely on a variety of sources, but the degree to which this is now possible with the aid of computers is much higher.

48. This corresponds to the debate between what Ronald Grimes has recently labeled the "supine" and "erect" schools of ritual and liturgical thinking. In the "supine" school (supine being characterized by flexibility and "closeness to the ground") ritual is seen as a fully cultural process, developing on the margins of a group, marked by inventiveness and creativity. The "erect" school (characterized by formality, repetitiveness, and authority) emphasizes the place of tradition, defines a class of essentials, and values the influence of the social and theological center as normative. See Ronald Grimes, "Liturgical Supinity, Liturgical Erectitude: On the Embodiment of Ritual Authority," in *Studia Liturgica* 23:1 (Spring, 1993).

49. Professional liturgists working in the area of liturgical revision are repeatedly warned by historians of the liturgy to save hard copies of all preliminary drafts of liturgical texts with the aim of allowing future historians of worship to reconstruct the decisions made in the revision process.

50. P. L. Berger, B. Berger, and H. Kellner, *The Homeless Mind* (New York: Vintage Books, 1973), p. 51. As early as 1911, sociologist Robert Michaels could refer to the trend toward bureaucratization as the "iron law" of modern society. *Political Parties: A Sociological Study of the Ologarchical Tendencies in Democracy* (New York: Free Press, 1967). See also Henry Jacoby, *The Bureaucratization of the World*, trans. by Evelyn

Kanes (Berkeley: University of California Press, 1973). Eugene Rochberg-Halton puts the case in a slightly more poetic way when he says: "The legacy of humanism (in its broadest sense) is a rationalized world and a de-humanized humanity—a Kafkaland where Calvin might wake from uneasy dreams à la Gregor Samsa of *The Metamorphosis*, to find himself and his legacy transformed into a giant bureaucracy" (*Meaning and Modernity: Social Theory and the Pragmatic Attitude* [Chicago: University of Chicago Press, 1986], p. 320).

51. Berger et al., *The Homeless Mind*, p. 50.

52. For the rapid rise of bureaucratic church structures in the twentieth century, see Robert Wuthnow, *The Restructuring of American Religion* (Princeton, N.J.: Princeton University Press, 1988), pp. 98-9; for similar developments in the Church of England, see Kenneth A. Thompson, *Bureaucracy and Church Reform, 1800-1965* (Oxford: Clarendon Press, 1970). One must also include in this category the interdenominational and ecumenical structures, which have proliferated in the past century.

53. Wuthnow, *The Restructuring of American Religion*, p. 126.

54. Berger et al., *The Homeless Mind*, p. 50. As early as 1882 church people began to comment upon this trend. In decrying the "over-organization of the churches," the *Nashville Christian Advocate* for June of that year makes the following forceful statement: "The church needs more power and not more machinery. It is a malign paradox of ecclesiastical history that, as power declines, machinery increases."

55. The Inter-Lutheran Commission on Worship was itself made up of representatives of worship bureaucracies from the Lutheran Church in America, the American Lutheran Church, the Evangelical Lutheran Church of Canada, and the Lutheran Church, Missouri Synod.

56. The work of Anthony Giddens, for example, in many ways presupposes a bureaucratized consciousness, but uses other categories to describe the impact of that consciousness on the individual self-in-society searching for meaning. See his *Modernity and Self-Identity: The Search for Meaning in the Late Modern Age* (Stanford, Stanford University Press, 1991).

57. Berger et al., *The Homeless Mind*, p. 50.

58. In his famous analysis of bureaucratic societies, Max Weber says that while these systems do indeed curtail individual creativity and personal initiative, they also ensure that decisions are made according to agreed-upon criteria and not on the whim of an individual. See Weber, *Economy and Society: An Outline of Interpretive Sociology* (Berkeley: University of California Press, 1978), pp. 956-60.

59. The frequent complaint about the Church of England *Alternative Service Book, 1980* that it seems uneven in tone and in quality is very much the result of differences in the various subcommittees that produced individual services and the failure to coordinate the work adequately. See R. C. D. Jasper *The Development of the Anglican Liturgy, 1662–1980* (London: SPCK, 1989).

60. Max Thurian, ed., *Churches Respond to BEM*, vol. III, Faith and Order Paper 135 (Geneva: World Council of Churches, 1987), pp. 85-86.

61. As a self-preservation strategy, many bureaucracies make the process of going outside the system more bureaucratically complex than working through it.

62. Some commentators say that bureaucracies make themselves intentionally incomprehensible, so that outsiders cannot penetrate the system and so that bureaucrats will be able to reject ideas from the outside as "unsuitable."

63. Within this middle ground we may note that there is a high correlation between the degree to which denominational traditions of public prayer are formalized and the degree to which denominational traditions of public prayer are bureaucratized. Roman Catholics, Anglicans, and Lutherans tend toward highly structured worship and institutional systems, while Baptists, Disciples of Christ, and others who tend toward minimal levels of liturgical formality also tend toward minimal levels of bureaucratization. There also seems to be a direct correlation between an increase in text-based, more stylized, and formalized worship patterns among Methodists (both in America and in the British Isles), Presbyterians, and the United Church of Christ and an increase in bureaucratic structures governing those worship patterns.

64. My first official act as a member of the Church of England Liturgical Commission, before I had attended a single meeting, was to sign a legal document relinquishing any right to patent or copyright any work I would do in conjunction with my duties for the Commission.

65. The growth and refinement of patent in the early decades of the twentieth century is traced by Thomas P. Hughes in *American Genesis: A Century of Invention and Technological Enthusiasm* (New York: Penguin, 1989), pp. 140-43. His description, *mutatis mutandis*, applies equally to the design and defense of copyright: "Patents . . . establish the boundaries of intellectual property. Inventors, like gold prospectors, spoke of staking out claims on the metes and bounds of their property. Patent lawyers defended against incursions, or infringements, within the field laid out. A well-designed patent covered as much territory as possible without infringing on another's property," (p. 142).

66. Basalla, *The Evolution of Technology* (Cambridge: Cambridge University Press, 1988), pp. 60-61.

67. Keith Watkins, ed., *Thankful Praise* (St. Louis, Mo.: CBP Press, 1987).

68. Ibid., p. 11.

69. Aidan Kavanagh, *On Liturgical Theology* (New York: Pueblo, 1988), pp. 7-8.

70. Ibid., p. 85.

71. Frederic L. Bender, "The Alienation of Common Praxis," in Gayle Ormiston, ed., *From Artifact to Habitat: Studies in the Critical Engagement of Technology* (London: Associated University Presses), pp. 155-174.

72. Berger et al., *The Homeless Mind*, p. 51.

73. *Critique of Dialectical Reason*, ed. Jonathan Ree (London: NLB, 1976), pp. 658-63. Sartre speaks here of bureaucracy as the "total suppression of the human."

74. Berger et al., *The Homeless Mind*, pp. 57-58.

75. Bender, "The Alienation of Common Praxis," in Ormiston, *From Artifact to Habitat*, p. 64. For Max Weber, the sociologist most identified with an analysis of bureaucracy, these sorts of faults with bureaucracy are far outweighed by its advantages.

76. Franz Neumann, *Behemoth: The Structure and Practice of National Socialism* (New York and London: Victor Gollancz, 1942), p. 368.

77. For a survey of reception as a contemporary ecumenical question see William G. Rusch *Reception: An Ecumenical Opportunity* (Philadelphia: Fortress, 1988). For the history of reception as a theological issue, see Edward J. Kilmartin, "Reception in History" in *The Search for Visible Unity*, ed. Jeffrey Gros (New York: Pilgrim Press, 1984), pp. 48-50. See also John Zizioulas, "The Theological Problem of Reception," *Centro pro Unione Bulletin* 26 (1984), p. 3.

78. Reception has also entered the vocabulary of literary criticism, and decribes the way in which a given literary text is received by the reader. In the work of some radical theorists, the very reality of a work is dependent upon its "reception" by the reader. This has been applied to biblical criticism by Bernard Lategan and William S. Vorster in *Text and Reality: Aspects of Reference in Biblical Texts* (Philadelphia: Fortress, 1985). The process of "reception" has been seen most recently in the responses to *Baptism, Eucharist, and Ministry*, Faith and Order Paper 111 and the discussions in local church councils of the various bilateral discussions.

79. William G. Rusch, *Reception: An Ecumenical Opportunity*. Reception can be a long and drawn-out process. It was only after fifty-six years of controversy that the decisions of the Council of Nicaea were generally received and endorsed by the Council of Chalcedon in 381.

80. Ibid., p. 43.

81. Kavanagh, *On Liturgical Theology*, p. 83.

82. As Ian Barbour explains, however, computers also have capacity the serve the cause of centralization: "Many institutional forces . . . favor the deployment of computers to strengthen hierarchical patterns of centralized control, but computers also present significant opportunities for decentralization.," *Ethics in an Age of Technology*, p. 155.

4. WORSHIP AND TECHNOLOGY IN HISTORY, 1

1. Roger Bacon, *Opus Majus*, vol. 1, trans. R. B. Burke (Philadelphia: University of Pennsylvania Press, 1928), p. 306. Bacon is especially noted for his visionary descriptions of the technology of the future. In 1260 he wrote: "Machines may be made by which the largest ships, with only one man steering them, will be moved faster than if they were filled with rowers; wagons may be built which will move with incredible speed and without the aid of beasts; flying machines can be constructed in which a man . . . may beat the air with wings like a bird. . . . Machines will make it possible to go to the bottom of seas and rivers." *De Secretis operibus*, cited in Lynn White Jr., *Medieval Technology and Social Change* (Oxford: Oxford University Press, 1962), p. 134.

2. Other historians place the end of this period slightly earlier, for example with the church's official condemnation of Roger Bacon in 1277. See, e.g. J. Gimpel, *The Medieval Machine: The Industrial Revolution in the Middle Ages* (London: Victor Gollancz, 1977).

3. Peter Abelard, theologian and philosopher (1079–1142); Robert Grosseteste, Bishop of Lincoln (1175?–1253), Bernard of Chartres, teacher, (?–1126?); Richard of Wallingford, Abbot of St. Albans (1292?–1335). Abbot Richard was a most interesting character indeed. He was a leper, the son of a blacksmith, and is credited with the invention of the first flying machine. He also designed and built a great *geometricum instrumentum* showing the movements of the sun, moon, and tides. In a contemporary Benedictine illumination, Abbot Richard is shown hammering on his machine at his forge, having tossed his mitre and crosier aside. See material on Richard in Lynn White Jr., "Medieval Engineering and the Sociology of Knowledge" in *Pacific Historical Review 44* (1975), pp. 1-21; and in Gimpel, *The Medieval Machine*, pp. 155-58. More will be said about Richard below. Bernard of Chartres was a famous pedagogue and scholar of Greek philosophy and literature, and has been traditionally credited with producing one of the earliest commentaries on the Æneid (although this is now being challenged by some scholars).

4. For a most useful table of the principal sources of ancient science translated in the Middle Ages, see J. Gimpel, *The Medieval Machine*, pp. 176-77.

5. Several social historians have correlated the increasing precision in instrumentation with increasing precision in systematic theology in the early medieval period. See Erwin Panofsky, *Gothic Architecture and Scholasticism* (New York, Meridian, 1957).

6. In a sermon given in 1306 in the Church of Santa Maria Novella in Florence, Fra Giordano says: "Not all the arts have been found: we shall never see an end of finding them. Every day one could discover a new art. . . . It is not twenty years since there was discovered the art of making spectacles which help one see well, an art which is one of the best and most necessary in the world. And that is such a short time ago that a new art which never before existed was invented . . . , I myself saw the man who discovered and practiced it and I talked with him." Quoted in Lynn White Jr. "Cultural Climates and Technological Advance in the Middle Ages," in *Viator* 2 (1971), p. 174.

7. Lynn White, "Medical Astrologers and Late-Medieval Technology," in *Medieval Religion and Technology* (Berkeley: University of California Press, 1977), p. 298.

8. Ibid., pp. 297-315; and on commerce and navigation see R. S. Lopez, *The Commercial Revolution of the Middle Ages, 950-1350* (Cambridge: Cambridge University Press, 1976).

9. Egypt seems to be the home of the first calendar, devised perhaps around 2800 B.C.E. Mesopotamia is also a suggested source location. They have in common a dependence on the flood stages of rivers. See, e.g., P. J. Huber, *Astronomical Dating of Babylon I and Ur III* (Malibu: Undena Publications, 1982) and the classic treatment by Stephen H. Langdon, *Babylonian Menologies and the Semitic Calendars*, Schweich Lectures, 1933 (London: Oxford University Press, 1934).

10. The Julian Calendar was based upon the assumption that the solar year is 365 1/4 days long, which is not precisely accurate. Such a calendar usually operates on a cycle of three 365-day years followed by one 366-day year. The annual discrepancy is about 11 minutes, which accumulates and puts the 21st of March increasingly later than the true vernal equinox.

11. See L. White, "Medieval Engineering and the Sociology of Knowledge," p. 16.

12. Ibid., p. 17.

13. The phrase belongs to R. W. Southern, in *The Making of the Middle Ages* (New Haven: Yale University Press, 1953), and others agree with his view that the monastic liturgy had salvific implications on a very large scale. For an alternative view see K. Halinger, "Zur geistigen Welt der Anfänge Klunys," in *Deutsches Archiv 10* (1954), pp. 417-45.

14. It was not only those in monasteries whose lives were ordered by the liturgical cycle. Eamon Duffy argues persuasively that, certainly until the Reformation, "For townsmen and countrymen alike, the rhythms of the liturgy . . . remained the rhythms of life itself." See Eamon Duffy, *Stripping the Altars, Traditional Religion in England, 1400-1580* (New Haven, Yale University Press, 1992), p. 52.

15. Bacon says: "At the beginning of the Church the winter solstice was placed on the eighth day before the Calends of January on the day of the Lord's nativity and the vernal equinox on the eighth day before the Calends of April. . . . For this year the winter solstice was on the Ides of December, twelve days before our Lord's nativity, and the vernal equinox on the third day before the Ides of March." *Opus Majus*, v. 1, p. 291.

16. *Opus Majus*, v. 1, pp. 290-96.

17. The astrolabe was an Arabic invention, first described in an illustrated treatise by al-Battani (d. 929 C.E.) in the early-tenth century. This is a geared instrument, a specimen of which survives from around 1220. The earliest Western astrolabe is probably from the late-twelfth century. See L. White, *Medieval Technology and Social Change*, pp. 122-23. See also Chaucer's *Treatise on the Astrolabe* (c. 1391).

18. Bacon, *Opus Majus*, vol. 1, p. 296.

19. Bacon had been asked by Pope Clement to dispatch to him an exposition of his system, which Bacon did in 1268. Unfortunately, Clement died in November of that year, without giving Bacon any commendation for his work.

20. Bacon, *Opus Majus*, pp. 311-12.

21. In that year, on March 7, 219 of Bacon's propositions were condemned by Stephen Tempier, Archbishop of Paris.

22. Quoted from John Leland (1506?–52), cited in Gimpel, *The Medieval Machine*, p. 158. The historian Thomas of Walsingham (1381?–1422?) describes the difficulties that Richard encountered when making his machine: "He made a noble work, a horologium, in the church, at a great cost of money and work; nor did he abandon finishing it because of its disparagement by the brethren, although they, wise in their own eyes, regarded it as the height of foolishness. . . . Indeed, when on a certain occasion the very illustrious King Edward the Third came to the monastery in order to pray, and saw the sumptuous work undertaken while the church was still not rebuilt since the ruin it suffered in Abbot Hugo's time, he discreetly rebuked Abbot Richard in that he neglected the fabric of the church and wasted so much money on a quite unnecessary work, namely the above-mentioned horologium. To which reproof the Abbot replied, with due respect, that enough Abbots would succeed him who would find workmen for the fabric of the monastery, but there would be no successor, after his death, who could finish the work that he had begun. And

indeed, he spoke the truth because in that art nothing of the kind remains, nor was anything similar invented in his lifetime." Cited in S. A. Bedini and F. R. Maddison, "Mechanical Universe: The Astrarium of Giovanni di Dondi," *Transactions of the American Philosophical Society* 56, part 5, October, 1966, pp. 6-7. (Thomas was educated at Oxford and was precentor and *scriptorius* of St. Albans from 1394.)

23. For more on d'Ailly, see Bernard Guenee, *Between Church and State: The Lives of Four French Prelates in the Late Middle Ages,* trans. Arthur Goldhammer (Chicago: University of Chicago Press, 1987).

24. Protestant countries were extremely unwilling to adopt the papal scheme, and as a result the Gregorian calendar was only adopted in England and America in 1752. The civil governments in many of the Orthodox countries were even slower to adopt the calendar, with Russia in 1918 and the pan–Orthodox Congress of Istanbul in 1923 the last. Various of the autocephalous Eastern Rite and Orthodox churches continue to follow the Julian calendar, and their fixed liturgical feasts are thirteen days later than in the Gregorian. The two Easters, and the feasts which depend on Easter, coincide about once every three years.

25. The World Calendar Association was founded mainly to further the ideas of Italian priest Marco Mastrofini, who in 1834 proposed a calendar scheme in which one day per year (two days in a leap year) would be outside any week or month. In Mastrofini's plan, every year would begin on the same day of the week, and Easter would be assigned a fixed date. The "World Calendar" is a refinement of this scheme, and for a brief period in the early 1950s the United Nations investigated its universal adoption. For a more detailed survey of the various twentieth-century calendar options, see Adolf Adam, *The Liturgical Year* (New York: Pueblo Press, 1981), pp. 289-302.

26. Ibid., p. 59.

27. The term *horologium* can be a little confusing in this period, in that it was applied to planetaria and clocks alike. See above note 22.

28. Lewis Mumford, *The Myth of the Machine* (New York: Harcourt, Brace Jovanovich, 1966), p. 286.

29. There are several histories of the clock, but the most important of these are J. D. North, "Monasticism and the First Mechanical Clocks," in *The Study of Time II,* ed. J. T. Fraser and N. Lawrence (New York: Springer-Verlag, 1975), pp. 381-98; Joseph Needham, Wang Ling, and Derek de Solla Price, *Heavenly Clock-work: The Great Astronomical Clocks of China* (Cambridge, Cambridge University Press, 1960); Carlo Cippola, *Clocks and Culture, 1300-1700* (London: Collins, 1967); and most recently David Landes, *Revolution in Time: Clocks and the Making of the Modern World* (Cambridge: Harvard University Press, 1983).

30. The normal course, and approximate times, of the Hours in a Benedictine monastery in winter was Nocturns (2:30 A.M.), Matins (5:00 A.M.), Prime (6:30 A.M.), Terce (8:15 A.M.), Sext (noon), None (2:15 P.M.), Vespers (4:15 P.M.), Compline (5:00 P.M.). Reading was done at 3:30, 5:45 A.M., 7:00 A.M., and 3:00 P.M., and work at 8:30 A.M. and 12:45 P.M. This was modified in different ways for the various seasons and feast days.

31. *The Rule of Saint Benedict,* trans. Abbot Parry, OSB (Leominster, U.K.: Gracewing, 1990), chap. 47: "The Signal for the Opus Dei." Any bell that was rung by a clock (a *clepsydra*) in this period seems to have rung only in order to awaken the person responsible for the ringing of the chapel bell. This person also seems to have been responsible for the adjustment of the clock each day to compensate for the unequal hours of day and night.

32. As late as the seventeenth century, instrument makers were testing mechanical clocks against the sundial and were devising sundials that gave readings accurate to the minute. See Landes, *Revolution in Time: Clocks and the Making of the Modern World,* pp. 121-22.

33. The water clock was basically a bowl with a hole in the bottom, which let out water at a specific rate, attached to a dial. These could be extraordinarily complex, however, with elaborate alarm mechanisms. Such a device was certainly used by the person in charge of seeing to it that the monks awoke for prayer in the night hours. The so-called "Moralized Bible" of the mid-thirteenth century has an illustration of 2 Kings 20:1-10 (where God adds fifteen years to the life span of Hezekiah) which shows God regulating a complex water clock with a weight-driven striking mechanism. See Lynn White, *Medieval Technology and Social Change,* p. 194, and illustration figure 3. For a good (if hypothetical) schematic diagram of a water clock, see Landes, *Revolution in Time: Clocks and the Making of the Modern World,* figure 2.

34. This poem, from a fragment of a drama called *Boeotia,* is attributed to the third-century B.C.E. playwright Plautus. Reprinted by permission of the publishers and the Loeb Classical Library from Plautus, Vols. 1-5, trans. Paul Nixon, Cambridge, Mass.: Harvard University Press, 1927.

35. See S. L. Macey, *Clocks and the Cosmos: Time in Western Life and Thought* (Hamden, Conn.: Archon, 1980), p. 22.

36. Benedict, *Rule,* chap. 10: "How the Praise of God Is to Be Carried Out in Summer."

37. There is in the medieval literature a genre composed of what post-Freudians would call "anxiety dreams" among monks concerned with missing prayers. "Peter the Venerable, Abbot of Cluny in the twelfth century, tells the story of Brother Alger, who woke thinking he had heard the bell ring for nocturns. Looking around, he thought he saw the other beds empty, so he drew on his sandals, threw on his cloak, and hastened to the chapel. There he was puzzled not to hear the sound of voices lifted in prayer. He hurried back to the dormitory. There he found all the other monks fast asleep. And then he understood: this was all a temptation of the devil, who had awakened him at the wrong time, so that when the bell for nocturns really rang, he would sleep through it." Landes, *Revolution in Time,* p. 65.

38. See Landes, *Revolution in Time,* p. 143, n. 3.

39. Most recent historians of technology agree that the mechanical clock was not a direct descendant of simpler water clocks and sundials, but from the *astraria* and *planetaria* of the thirteenth century. "Clearly," says Lynn White, "the origins of the mechanical clock lie in a complex realm of monumental planeteria, equitoria, and geared astrolabes." (*Medieval Religion and Technology,* p. 123). This thesis was most powerfully advanced by Derek de Solla Price who states that "the mechanical clock

is naught but a fallen angel from the world of astronomy." Price, "Clockwork before the Clock" in *The Horological Journal* 97 (December, 1955), p. 810. Landes quite strongly disagrees with this, and gives clocks and timekeeping by the clock, an independent status and developmental track. See Landes, *Revolution in Time: Clocks and the Making of the Modern World*, chap. 3.

40. Lynn White, *Medieval Religion and Technology*, p. 124.

41. The word *clock* is derived from the German *Glocke* meaning bell. The earliest mechanical clocks were indeed simply automated bells that struck at regular intervals.

42. Gimpel, *The Medieval Machine*, pp.168-69.

43. This was by order of a bull of Pope Sabinianus in the seventh century.

44. Gimpel, *The Medieval Machine*, p. 169.

45. Ibid., p. 71. There was, however, in a separate building outside the Hagia Sophia in Constantinople, a small building containing a sundial and a *clepsydra*. See Lynn White, *Medieval Religion and Technology*, p. 249. The Greek Church also forbade in its liturgy another of the great technological innovations of the medieval period, the pipe organ. Neither, it seems, did Orthodox priests wear wrist-watches until relatively recently.

46. Ibid., p. 249. Quite abruptly, there is an increase in the literary references to clocks, beginning in the early years of the fourteenth century. Because clocks involved both expense and upkeep, they appear with frequency in cathedral and monastery records, and a new profession, the *horologeur* (or clock maker) begins to be recorded.

47. By the end of this period, the machinery of the clock so dominated monastic life that Mumford could say that "the monasteries *were machines*. The regimentation necessary to run the 'well-tempered monastery', where each person had a function and each function had a time and season was a 'machine phenomenon' " (Mumford, *Technics and Civilization*, p. 41). The cardinal virtue "Temperance" from the mid-fifteenth century begins to appear iconographically associated with a clock. Indeed, it is from these early images of Temperance that much of what we know about early clock mechanisms has been derived. In about 1400, the writer Christine de Pisan (c. 1362–c. 1429) describes her vision of Temperance: "Temperance should be called a goddess also. And because our human body is made up of many parts and should be regulated by reason, it may be represented as a clock in which there are several wheels and measures. And just as the clock is worth nothing unless it is regulated, so our human body does not work unless Temperance orders it" (in White, "Temperantia and the Virtuousness of Technology" in *Medieval Religion and Technology*, p. 194). Christine, an almost exact contemporary of Jean d'Arc, is a fascinating character in her own right. The daughter of Charles V's astrologer, as a young child she showed extraordinary gifts in language and, later, in historiography. See Enid McLeod, *The Order of the Rose: The Life and Ideas of Christine de Pizan* (London: Chatto and Windus, 1976); Angus J. Kennedy, *Christine de Pisan: A Bibliographical Guide* (London: Grant and Cutler, 1984).

48. Landes, *Revolution in Time: Clocks and the Making of the Modern World*, p. 78.

49. Samuel Butler, *Erewhon: Or Over the Range*, rev. ed. (London: A. C. Fifield, 1908). Perhaps the most gripping and frightening vision of the human toll exacted by living life by the clock is Fritz Lang's 1926 film classic *Metropolis*. In one heavily allegorical sequence, the hero Freders, the son of the master of Metropolis, has entered the underground machine world ("The Depths"), which maintains and regulates life in Metropolis. Disguising himself as a worker, Freders takes charge of working the hands on the giant clock that orders both human and mechanized work. After hours of backbreaking toil we see Freders hanging on the hands of the clock, arms outstretched, and crying out "Father, will these ten hours never end!?"

50. The phrase belongs to Lewis Mumford, whose 1934 analysis of the impact of the clock remains valid. See *Technics and Civilization*, especially chap. 2.

51. "Perhaps the earliest recorded example of the new, secular time standard comes to us from Sarum, England [Salisbury], where a regulation of 1306 stated that 'before the clock of the Cathedral had struck one, no person was to purchase or cause to be purchased flesh, fish, or other victuals.' " Landes, *Revolution in Time: Clocks and the Making of the Modern World*, p. 77.

52. Roy Rappaport, "Ritual, Time, and Eternity" *Zygon* 27:1 (March 1992), p. 25.

53. Landes, *Revolution in Time: Clocks and the Making of the Modern World*, p. 78.

5. WORSHIP AND TECHNOLOGY IN HISTORY, 2

1. The first recorded use of the term is in 1947, and refers to what we would now call human mechanics or "kinesthetics." The use of the word in its modern sense is first found in 1969 in the June issue of *Science Journal*.

2. See Henry Rack, *Reasonable Enthusiast*, 2nd ed. (Nashville: Abingdon Press, 1992), p. 361.

3. See Wesley's *Primitive Physic* (London, 1747). This extraordinary treatise contains treatment suggestions for hundreds of ailments, with remedies ranging from "goose-dung" to "rotten apples" proposed. The recommendation that a patient "be electrified daily" is often found. Wesley says, "I am firmly persuaded there is no remedy in nature for nervous disorders of every kind comparable to the proper use of the Electrical Machine" (p. 69). Mainly it was nervous disorders that called for shock treatment, but it was also advised for "falling sickness," "head-ach" [*sic*], bruises and burns, cramps, and shingles. However, Wesley always said that the "sovereign remedy" was prayer.

4. Miasmas are also occasionally referred to as "mephitic vapors" in this period.

5. John Macculloch, *Malaria: An Essay* (London, 1827), p. 18.

6. See Ruth Richardson, *Death, Dissection, and the Destitute* (London: Penguin, 1988), pp. 60-63. The population of the city of Leeds, for example, had risen from about 6,000 in 1700 to 43,602 in 1821. Cities on the Continent and in the United States experienced similar population explosions in this period. Owen Chadwick describes the situation in *The Victorian Church* (London: A. and C. Black, 1971): "Nothing in the cities was equipped to cope. Municipal government, building, sanitation, health, cemeteries, hospitals, roads, paving, lighting, police, dentists,

schools—all the organs of public life were strained until they were bursting" (p. 325). In villages the cemetery overcrowding situation was less acute, and in many cities and towns charnel houses had been built to "receive the bones of those found when the ground was reused before decay was complete." See J. Morgan "The Burial Question in Leeds in the Eighteenth and Nineteenth Centuries" in Ralph Houl-brooke, *Death, Ritual, and Bereavement* (London: Routledge, 1989), p. 95.

7. The increasing use of common pit burials for the indigent, and especially those resident in workhouses, added to the situation. Thomas Pennant, writing in the 1790s, describes the conditions in the graveyard of St. Giles-in-the-Fields. "In the church-yard I have observed with horror a square pit, with many rows of coffins piled one upon the other, all exposed to sight and smell. Some of the piles were incomplete, expecting the mortality of the night. I turned away disgusted with the view, and scandalized at the want of police, which so little regards the health of the living as to permit so many putrid corpses, tacked between some slight boards, dispersing their effluvia all over the capital." Cited in Richardson, *Death, Dissection, and the Destitute*, p. 60. See also Chris Brooks, *Mortal Remains* (Exeter: Wheaton, 1989), pp. 3-8, and Dr. George Alfred Walker's influential *Gatherings from Grave-yards* (London, 1839). Walker called for "the enforcement of Sanatory [sic] regulations" and "THE ENTIRE REMOVAL OF THE DEAD FROM THE PROX-IMITY OF THE LIVING."

8. Owen Chadwick, *The Victorian Church*, p. 327.

9. See R. J. Morris, *Cholera, 1832* (London: Croom Helm, 1976); M. Durey, *The Return of the Plague* (Dublin, 1979); and N. Longmate, *King Cholera* (London, 1966). In 1832, Parliament had addressed another burial problem with a biotech-nological root by enacting the Anatomy Act and New Poor Law. The flourishing of schools of anatomy in the various cities around Britain resulted in the need for large numbers of bodies for dissection. Although a law had been passed in the reign of Henry VIII that allowed judges to give over to the anatomists the bodies of certain persons executed for murder, a limit of six per year was imposed, leaving the increasing need of the anatomy schools unmet by legal means. From the last quarter of the eighteenth century, gangs of body snatchers (also known as "resurrectionists") found a ready market for as many bodies as they could supply. The corpses of the poor were particularly at risk, not only because of the prevalence of pit burials (see note 7), but also because, unlike the wealthy, they could not afford such preventive measures as guards, patented lead coffins, and private secured burial sites. The new legislation left the bodies of the poor even more vulnerable to dissection, since it allowed anatomists to take unclaimed bodies or the bodies of those who were unable to pay funeral expenses. Generally, these were the impoverished residents of workhouses, hospitals, asylums, or prisons. The background (and gross injustice) of this act are explored by Ruth Richardson in her learned and fascinating book *Death, Dissection, and the Destitute*.

10. *Punch*, Autumn, 1849. "An Elegy Written in a London Churchyard." Thirteen years earlier, in 1836, A. W. N. Pugin had contrasted the dignity and sanctity of a medieval burial with the chaos and sacrilege of contemporary practice in *Contrasts*.

(He also criticized the treatment of the poor in modern times by showing the body of a workhouse resident being carted away for dissection purposes. See note 9.)

11. Stannard, *Death in America* (Philadelphia: University of Pennsylvania Press, 1976), p. 74. Similar conditions prevailed in western Europe and especially in France, see Philippe Ariès, *The Hour of Our Death* (New York: Knopf, 1981), 348-50, 479-88, and 540-41. During this same period, the city itself became something of a "technological problem" with issues of population control, waste management, transportation, and overall city planning beginning to be addresses in systematic ways. Lewis Mumford, *The City in History* (London: Secker and Wartburg, 1961).

12. Chris Brooks, *Mortal Remains* (Exeter: Wheaton, 1989), p. 2. It was not until 1852, with the passage by Parliament of the first Burials Act, that Nonconformists were permitted to bury according to their own rites in urban and rural churchyards.

13. For a description of the difficulties with burial fees in this period, see J. Morgan in Ralph Houlbrooke, *Death, Ritual, and Bereavement,* pp. 97-99. For the wider dimensions of this controversy, see Owen Chadwick, *The Victorian Church,* pp. 60-95.

14. These alternative provisions by Nonconformist chapels are described by Morgan as "small and unimportant." Morgan, in Houlbrooke, *Death, Ritual, and Bereavement,* p. 95.

15. *Punch,* Autumn, 1849. "An Elegy Written in a London Churchyard."

16. For Père Lachaise as a model of other garden cemeteries of the era, see S. French "The Cemetery as a Cultural Institution" in Stannard, *Death in America,* pp. 85-89. See also C. Brooks, *Mortal Remains,* pp. 7-8, and Ariès, *The Hour of Our Death,* pp. 531-36. Of the "magnificent seven" London suburban cemeteries (Highgate, Brompton, Kensal Green, Norwood, Abney Park, Nunhead, Tower Hamlets), High-gate was surely the most significant. By the time it was closed in 1975, 166,800 people had been buried in 51,800 graves and catacombs. They included Karl Marx, George Eliot, and Dante Gabriele Rossetti.

17. The suburban-park-cemetery ideal traveled westward across America, and in 1917 what is perhaps the apotheosis of such cemeteries was built: Forest Lawn in Los Angeles, designed and built by Hubert Eaton. Landscape architect J. C. Louden, in his 1843 article "On the Laying-out, Planting, and Managing of Cemeteries" writes that his goal is to plan a cemetery in order that "the disposal of the remains of the dead [might be accomplished] in such a manner that their decomposition and return to the earth shall not prove injurious to the living either by affecting health nor by shocking feelings, opinions, and prejudices," in *Gardeners Magazine,* 1843. Cited in Peter Jupp, *From Dust to Ashes: The Replacement of Burial by Cremation in England, 1840–1967* (London: Congregational Memorial Hall Trust, 1990), p. 5. The Cambridge-Camden Society had much to say about the design of cemetery chapels, arguing that the most appropriate model was a version of the Church of the Holy Sepulchre in Jerusalem. See Gilbert Cope, ed., *Dying, Death, and Disposal* (London: SPCK, 1970), pp. 53-54.

18. In one of its most strenuous calls for liturgical reform, the Cambridge-Camden Society argued that the fashionable funeral procession was "pagan" in its essence, and published a series of articles in *The Ecclesiologist* condemning the "atheistical

character of funeral processions. . . . These modern inventions are even worse than the old kind of burials, with their kid gloves, and seed cake, and feathers, and the 'funeral pue.' " *The Ecclesiologist*, 1845. Quoted in G. Cope, *Death, Dying, and Disposal*, p. 51. By 1851 the Society's views had developed significantly on this issue and they published a tract *Funerals and Funeral Arrangements* consisting of articles that had previously appeared in the *Ecclesiologist*. "Let us get rid of the expensive trash of a modern funeral," they demanded. *Funerals and Funeral Arrangements*, p. 10.

19. Ruth Richardson, "Why Was Death so Big in Victorian Britain?" in Houlbrooke, *Death, Ritual, and Bereavement*, p. 111. The publicity surrounding the funerals of important persons such as the Duke of Wellington and Abraham Lincoln also had a profound effect on shaping public taste in funerals. An estimated "£80,000 changed hands for seats [for Wellington's] funeral." Ibid., p. 185.

20. The classic work on the development of the funeral industry is Jessica Mitford's *The American Way of Death* (New York: Simon and Schuster, 1963). See also Robert Habenstein and William Lamers, *The History of American Funeral Directing* (Milwaukee: Bulfin, 1962). Richardson also points out that the elaborate funerals devised by Friendly Societies, trade unions, and fraternal organizations had a profound impact on public taste in the nineteenth century.

21. Instituted in August 1850. Technically "An Act to make better Provision for the Interment of the Dead in and near the Metropolis." This Act was preceded by a Public Health Act in 1848 and followed by two additional cemeteries' regulation acts in 1852 and 1853.

22. Peter Jupp calls the movement from churchyard to suburban cemetery the "greatest change in the disposal of the dead in England for over 1000 years." Jupp, *From Dust to Ashes*, p. 8. Surprisingly, that great promoter of all things medieval, the Cambridge Camden Society, supported this move to extramural burial grounds and for the provision of municipal cemeteries. Under their plan, part of this ground would be consecrated by the church, the rest left for dissenters, but "the two parts should be as distinct as if they were two separate grounds." *Funerals and Funeral Arrangements*, p. 27. See also J. F. White, *The Cambridge Movement*, p. 215.

23. Morgan, in *Death, Ritual, and Bereavement*, p. 100.

24. G. Rowell, *The Liturgy of Christian Burial*, Alcuin Club Collections 59 (London: SPCK, 1977), p. 64.

25. In the *Genevan Service Book* (1556), John Knox has simplified the rite to the point that the only ceremony is that "the corps is reverently brought to the grave, accompanied by the congregation withe owte any further ceremonies."

26. In Cranmer's 1552 *Book of Common Prayer*, although there is a rubric about "proceeding to the Church," the directions for which part of the service, if any, is to be said in the church and which at the grave are ambiguous. One of the stated aims of the 1662 service was to clear up this ambiguity.

27. Ariès, *The Hour of Our Death*, p. 496.

28. *The Book of Common Prayer with the Additions and Deviations Proposed in 1928* (London, 1928).

29. John 1:25-6; Job 19:25-27; and a collation of 1 Timothy 6:7 and Job 1:21.

30. Psalms 34 and 90 and 1 Corinthians 15:41-58. A charmingly emphatic rubric opens the burial service in 1904: "We will on no account whatever make a charge for burying the dead."

31. Liturgy Office of the Bishops' Conference of England and Wales, *Order of Christian Funerals* (London: Geoffrey Chapman, 1991).

32. Wheatley, *The Church of England Man's Companion, or a Rational Illustration of the Harmony . . . and Usefulness of the Book of Common Prayer,* 1710, p. 467. This sentiment was also expressed by those designing suburban garden cemeteries a century-and-a-half later. J. C. Louden states that in addition to providing a healthier way to dispose of the dead, "A secondary is, or ought to be, the improvement of the moral sentiments and general taste of all classes and most especially of the great masses of society." (Cited by G. Rowell "Nineteenth-Century Attitudes" in Cope, *Dying, Death, and Disposal,* p. 54.)

33. Eamon Duffy describes the situation in late-medieval England, when "funerals . . . were intensely concerned with the notion of community in which living and dead were not separated, in which the bonds of affection, duty, and blood continued to bind." *The Stripping of the Altars: Traditional Religion in England, c. 1400–c.1580* (New Haven: Yale, 1992), p. 475. A secondary change to be noted here is the improvement in refrigeration techniques which, when exploited by the funeral industry, diminished the practice of keeping the body at home and the rites of watching and waking which traditionally attended it. See above p. 79.

34. Jupp, *From Dust to Ashes,* p. 27.

35. Louden, "The Laying-out, Planting, and Managing of Cemeteries." See p. 151, n. 17.

36. J. Morgan, "The Burial Question in Leeds in the Eighteenth and Nineteenth Centuries" in R. Houlbrooke, *Death, Ritual, and Bereavement,* pp. 103-4.

37. R. Houlbrooke, "Death, Church and Family in England between the late-15th and early-18th Centuries," in R. Houlbrooke, *Death, Ritual, and Bereavement,* p. 35.

38. The first quotation from the *Book of Common Prayer,* 1662 and the second from "A Service of Death and Resurrection," *The United Methodist Hymnal,* 1989.

39. See Richardson, *Death, Dissection, and the Destitute,* chap. 1. Many other household rites have similarly disappeared, but the history of this trend has yet to be written.

40. Jupp, *From Dust to Ashes,* p. 9.

41. R. Hovda, "Reclaiming for the Church the Death of a Christian, I" in *Worship* 59:2 (March, 1985), p. 149.

42. Even coffins have gone "high-tech." A recent advertisement in one of the funeral industry's professional journals advertised the "Monarch Deluxe," a wooden coffin with music piped in through special speakers and a new type of hermetic seal. The motto of the company that offered this coffin was "All the warmth that wood can give." Philippe Ariès attributes much of the strength of the elaborate, professionalized American funeral to the increased technologization of death in the United States. With life artificially prolonged in hospitals, and the dying placed outside of the context of normal family life, "it is necessary to devise a period of contemplation and solemnity between death and burial." "The Reversal of Death" in Stannard, *Death in America,* p. 155.

43. See James F. White and Susan J. White, *Church Architecture* (Nashville: Abingdon, 1988), chap. 9. Of the comments that were received by the authors in response to their suggestion that new church planning might consider the provision of burial space, most expressed deep concern that sanitation codes and hygiene sensitivity would be violated. See also R. Hovda, "Reclaiming for the Church the Death of a Christian, II" in *Worship* 59:3 (May, 1985), pp. 251-61.

44. There are several useful surveys of the history of the Temperance Movement, including Norman Clark, *Deliver us from Evil: an Interpretation of American Prohibition* (New York: Norton, 1976), John Kobler, *Ardent Spirits: The Rise and Fall of Prohibition* (London: Michale Joseph, 1973); Jack S. Blocker Jr. *American Temperance Movements: Cycles of Reform* (Boston: Twayne, 1989); Ian Tyrell, *Sobering Up* (Westport, Conn.: Greenwood Press, 1979; for the progress of temperance in England see Brian Harrison, *Drink and the Victorians: The Temperance Question in England, 1815–1872* (London, 1971).

45. Preached at Hanover Street Church, Boston on the first 6 Sundays of 1826, and cited in Kobler, *Ardent Spirits*, p. 54. Following Beecher's sermons, in that same year, New England Christians formed the American Society for the Promotion of Temperance.

46. "They believed that in normal, sensible use, fermented drinks were not *in fact* intoxicating. This was a folk wisdom fixed as early as the American conscience as when Increase Mather had preached to the Puritans 'the wine is from God' but had warned them sternly that 'the drunkard is from the Devil.'" Clark, *Deliver Us from Evil*, p. 9.

47. See Jack S. Blocker Jr., *American Temperance Movements*, pp. 22-23.

48. The New York State Temperance Society endorsed teetotalism in 1835, and in 1836 the American Temperance Union followed suit. Clark argues that teetotalism and prohibition were not so much designed to protect the individual from drink, but rather were a response to the growth of the bourgeois family ideal, and that "protecting the American home" became the primary motivation. Clark, *Deliver Us from Evil*, pp. 43-44.

49. Prohibition in the United States was in force from 1919 to the repeal of the amendment in 1933.

50. Thomas B. Welch, "What Wine Shall we Use at the Lord's Supper?," (privately published, 1870).

51. See O. Chadwick, *The Victorian Church*, for a description of such a schism in Penzance and St. Ives: "In 1837-1838 The Methodists of Penzance and St. Ives adopted teetotalism as a gospel. They began to desert worship led by ministers who would not sign the pledge and to demand sacraments with unfermented wine. Conference of 1841 prohibited unfermented wine, and closed the chapels to any but teetotal meetings. They were not in sympathy with local zeal. A prudent Cornish superintendent prevented worse schism by allowing the chapels to Penzance teetotalers and by turning a blind eye to some use of unfermented wine. But by 1842 there was a group of about six hundred separated from Conference and organized as the Teetotal Wesleyan Methodists," p. 378.

52. Blocker, *American Temperance Movements*, p. 24.

53. Ibid., pp. 24-25.

54. Large numbers of tracts outlining the biblical aspects of the "communion wine question" were produced in the 1860s and 1870s by adherents to all denominations from Protestant Episcopalians to Swedenborgians. They bear titles such as "The Divine Law as to Wines, Established by the Testimony of the Sages: Conformed by Their Provision of Unfermented Wines for Medicinal and Sacramental Use" (1880), "What Is Scripture Wine?" (1864), and "Gospel Temperance: The Law of God" (1878). Many Temperance Christians rallied under the banner of Jeremiah 35:5-6, 14: "And I set before the sons of the house of the Rechabites pots full of wine, and cups, and I said unto them, Drink ye wine. But they said, We will drink no wine: for Jonadab the son of Rechab our father commanded us, saying, Ye shall drink no wine, neither ye, nor your sons forever. The words of Jonadab the son of Rechab, that he commanded his sons not to drink wine, are performed; for until us this day they drink none, but obey their father's commandment" (KJV). The Independent Order of Rechabites, a secretive fraternal organization, was one of the first American temperance societies to advocate total abstinence. Other texts cited were Proverbs 20:1, 23:31; and Isaiah 5:22.

55. In 1860, in order to support efforts to restrict the traffic in alcohol conference passed a resolution that stated, "We highly approve of the growing practice among our brethren of supplying themselves with domestic wine for the sacrament." Methodist Episcopal Church *Journal*, 1860, pp. 394-95.

56. At the same time, the wider temperance movement saw the continued use of alcohol at communion as a serious obstacle to their work. The National Temperance Convention that met in Saratoga in August, 1865, adopted the following resolution: "Resolved, that should all Christian churches confine themselves to [unfermented wine] at the table of the Lord, it would remove one of the strongest pleas for the necessity and morality of the intoxicating traffic, and one of the chief supports to the pretended innocence and divine sanction of intoxicating drinks." For an impressive survey of Methodist regulations on the consumption of alcohol, see Ivan Blackwell Bennett Jr., *Methodism and Alcohol: Recommendations for a Beverage Alcohol Policy based on the Ever-changing Historic Disciplinal Positions of American Methodism* (Claremont: unpublished D.Min. thesis, 1973). See also on this subject George Thompson Brake, *Drink: Ups and Downs of Methodist Attitudes toward Temperance* (London: Oliphants, 1974). The fact that the energies of many Christians were devoted to the abolition of slavery may account for the fact that vigorous attention was paid to temperance only after the War. Drink was described as the "new slavery," as in the National Prohibition Party's first official platform in 1869: "Slavery is gone, but drunkenness! . . . The lot of the literal slave, of him whom others enslaved, is indeed a hard one; nevertheless, it is paradise compared with the lot of him, who has enslaved himself—especially of him who has enslaved himself to alcohol." Cited in Kobler, *Ardent Spirits*, p. 111.

57. *Minutes of the New York East Annual Conference*, p. 24 (Section 6: "Report on Temperance").

58. *Minutes of the New York Annual Conference, 1872*, Section 8, p. 35. The minutes of the New York East Conference for 1871 record that the delegates "earnestly

recommend and exhort the Stewards of our churches, to whom the providing of our Sacraments belongs, that they use all possible carefulness to provide such wines as shall afford no element or shadow of endorsement of one of the greatest scourges that blast the human race." *Minutes*, p. 37.

59. Ibid., p. 68.

60. For example, in 1868, The New York East Annual Conference resolves "That we will use unintoxicating wine for sacramental purposes, *as far as we are able to procure it*" (emphasis added).

61. For helpful surveys of Pasteur's work, see Bruno Latour, *The Pasteurization of France* (Cambridge: Harvard University Press, 1988), J. Nicholle, *Louis Pasteur: A Master of Scientific Enquiry*, (Hammondsworth, U.K.: Pelican, 1969), and J. D. Bernal, *Science in History: The Scientific and Industrial Revolutions*, vol. 2, 3rd ed. (New York: A. R. Liss, 1986).

62. L. Pasteur, "On the Organized Bodies which Exist in the Atmosphere: Examination of the Doctrine of Spontaneous Generation," 1861. This important treatise posits the omnipresence of microbes, outlines the theory and practice of sterilization, and argues for the abandonment of the theory of the spontaneous generation of disease agents.

63. J. Gregory Zeikus, "Fermentation and Anaerobiosis" in H. Koprowski and S. A. Plotkin, *The World's Debt to Pasteur* (Proceedings of a Centennial Symposium Commemorating the First Rabies Vaccination, January 17-18, 1985).

64. He was engaged by Napoleon III to uncover the sources of "wine maladies," and published his results in 1866 as "Etudes sur le Vin." See M. A. Amerine, "Wine-Making" in Koprowski and Plotkin, *The World's Debt to Pastuer*, pp. 67-81.

65. The word *pasteurization* for the process of sterilization of foods was first used in Germany in 1871.

66. Townsend ("Communion Wine and Bible Temperance") is arguing that each time the Bible speaks of wine, it is referring to unfermented wine. His argument rests on the use of unfermented wine at the Passover, and he uses quotations from ancient and contemporary Rabbinic sources in support. Cyril, Jerome, Clement, Origen, and Basil are all cited as advocating unfermented wine at the Eucharist.

67. "As Pasteur has shown, the motes in the air can be collected on cotton or asbestos placed in a tube through which air has been drawn" (Townsend, "Communion Wine and Bible Temperance," p. 192).

68. Ibid., p. 203.

69. Ibid., p. 224.

70. See William Chazanof, *Welch's Grape Juice: From Cooperation to Cooperative* (Syracuse: Syracuse University Press, 1977).

71. Welch also devised "Dr. Welch's Sistem of Simplified Spelling" and began work on a dictionary using his "sistem."

72. C. E. Welch, "Last Will and Testament," cited in Chazanof, p. 1. Chazanof says "The grapes were cooked for a few minutes, the juice squeezed through cloth bags, and the remaining grape liquid filtered into a few bottles standing on the kitchen table. Dr. Tom now plugged the bottles with cork and wax and immersed the decanters up to their necks in boiling water. The bottles remained in this position

for what T[homas]. B[ramwell]. [Welch] hoped would be long enough to destroy the yeast organisms in the juice and thus preventing fermentation." In 1869 the first bottles of "Dr. Welch's Unfermented Wine" was offered for sale.

73. Having come under the influence of Bishop William Taylor, the younger Welch was prepared to set sail for Africa in 1886 as a self-supporting missionary, but was discouraged by his family for reasons of both health and economics, since he was then in charge of the grape juice firm. He decided to devote his efforts to home-based support of the African mission, and edited the *African News* for some time.

74. Chazanof, *Welch's Grape Juice*, p. 76.

75. Ibid., p. 77.

76. Each denomination has its own history of debate over the issue of communion wine. See Bennett, *Methodism and Alcohol*. For example, in 1912 the Reverend Mark Matthews, then moderator of the Presbyterian General Assembly and pastor of the largest Presbyterian congregation in the world, galvanized religious opinion against the liquor trade by calling it "the most fiendish, corrupt and hell-soaked institution that ever crawled out of the slime of the eternal pit." Harrison, *Drink and the Victorians*, p. 4.

77. Richard J. Jensen, *The Winning of the Midwest: Social and Political Conflict, 1888-1896* (Chicago: University of Chicago Press, 1971). Jensen points out that these divisions were more important than ethnic or cultural identities—that is, German Catholics were more likely to ally themselves politically with Irish Catholics than with German Methodists.

78. In 1888, the Lambeth Conference met and addressed the question of communion wine. "Resolved: that the Bishops assembled in this Conference declare that the use of unfermented juice of the grape or any liquid other than true wine, diluted or undiluted, as the element in the administration of the cup in the Holy Communion, is unwarranted by the example of Our Lord and is an unauthorized departure from the custom of the Catholic Church." For a good summary of the historical reasons behind the Anglican-Methodist divide on the issue of drink, see J. P. K. Byrnes "A Study of the Differences Between the Anglican and Methodist Churches on such Questions as Drink and Gambling" in W. S. F. Pickering, ed., *Anglican-Methodist Relations: Some Institutional Factors,* Papers presented to the Study Commission on Institutionalism, Commission on Faith and Order, World Council of Churches (London: Dartman, Longman, and Todd, 1961), pp. 166-70.

79. *Report of the Anglican-Methodist Unity Commission: Part 2, The Scheme* (London, SPCK, 1968). "The Use of Fermented Wine" is discussed in paragraphs 185-192.

80. Ibid., p. 61.

81. The parallel Report on Anglican-Methodist Union in Wales (1965) adds that this process had been recently imported from Germany.

82. Ibid., paragraph 191, p. 63.

83. The Institut Pasteur itself was cautious in this period, issuing the following warning: "But we should maintain a certain reserve for the time being and not see bacteria everywhere, after previously seeing them nowhere." Cited in Bruno Latour, *The Pasteurization of France*, p. 117.

84. This too had ecumenical implications. The report on Anglican-Methodist Union in Wales says under the heading "Some Differences in [Eucharistic] Practice": "It was noted that . . . the use of many individual cups in some Methodist Churches seems to Anglicans to weaken the proper symbolism of the One Cup . . . " (paragraph 32, p. 58).

85. Quite recently I was shown an advertisement for a sanitary individual communion distribution system, consisting of individual plastic cups in an hourglass shape, sealed top and bottom. Each member of the congregation is expected to collect one of these at the church door, and at the appropriate time to break the seal at the bottom to release a small piece of bread and then to break the seal at the top to expose a dose of wine.

86. "The General Instruction" in the *Roman Missal* says: "The sign of communion is more complete when given under both kinds, since in that form the sign of the eucharistic meal appears more clearly. . . . The faithful should be urged to take part in the rite which brings out the sign of the eucharistic meal more fully" (nos. 240, 241).

87. When the return to distribution of the elements in both kinds was being debated among Roman Catholics, the question of the chalice as a means of disease-transmission was put to the American Medical Association which declared that wiping and turning a chalice between communicants "seems to remove any danger." *Bishops' Committee on the Liturgy Newsletter* 15 (January, 1979), p. 147. Studies by William Burrows and Elizabeth S. Hemmers (first published in the *Journal of Infectious Diseases*) concluded that "Experiments on the transmission of test organisms from one person to another by the common use of the chalice showed that approximately 0.001 percent of the organisms are transferred even under the most favorable conditions; and when conditions approximated those of actual use, no transmission could be detected." See also Robert W. Hovda, "AIDS Hysteria and the Common Cup: Take and Drink" in *Worship* 60:1 (1986), pp. 67-73, who concludes from all available evidence that, "The things we know about AIDS simply do not support any misgivings about holy communion from the common plate and the common cup" p. 72.

6. LITURGY AND MECHANIZATION

1. Thomas Carlyle, "The Mechanical Age" ("Signs of the Times," *Edinburgh Review* [June, 1829], p. 442). Charles Darwin says something similar about the state of his own mind when he says "I have said that in one respect my mind has changed in the last twenty or thirty years. Up to the age of thirty, poetry of many kinds . . . gave me great pleasure, and even as a schoolboy I took intense delight in Shakespeare. But now for many years I cannot read a line of poetry; I have tried lately to read Shakespeare, and found it so intolerably dull that it nauseated me. I have also almost lost my taste for pictures or music. . . . My mind seems to have become a kind of machine for grinding general laws out of a large collection of facts." "Recollections of the Development of My Mind and Character," written in 1881 and printed in Francis Darwin, ed. *The Life and Letters of Charles Darwin* (London: John Murray,

1887). Carlyle, "The Mechanical Age," p. 443, says of the society as a whole, "Were we required to characterize this age of ours by any single epithet, we should be tempted to call it, not an Historical, Devotional, Philosophical, or Moral Age, but above all others, the Mechanical Age. It is the Age of Machinery, in every outward and inward sense of that word: the age which, with its whole undivided might, forwards, teaches and practices the great art of adapting means to ends."

2. Although René Descartes specifically objected to conceiving a human being as a machine in the *Discourse on Method, V,* less than one hundred years later LaMettrie (1709–1751) opposed this view vigorously in *L'Homme Machine,* in which he describes human physical activities as mechanical functions of the brain. See Lewis W. Spitz, "Model Man, Modern Man, Reformation Man" in L. Spitz, ed., *Continuity and Discontinuity in History Essays presented in honor of George Hunstan Williams* (Leiden: Brill, 1979), pp. 381-82.

3. Karl Marx, *Grundrisse: Foundations of the Critique of Political Economy* (London: Pelican, 1973), p. 171.

4. In his important work of social analysis, *The Myth of the Machine* (New York: Harcourt Brace Jovanovich, 1966), Lewis Mumford explores the impact of machine thinking on human consciousness.

5. Ibid., p. 294.

6. G. Claudin, *Paris* (Paris, 1867), pp. 1-2. Cited in Schivelbusch, *The Railway Journey* (Berkeley: University of California Press, 1977), p. 159. See also J. L. Casti, *Paradigms Lost: Images of Man in the Mirror of Science* (New York: Morrow, 1989).

7. The question of whether or not, in Carlyle's words, we are indeed "grown mechanical in head and heart, as well as in hand" continues to be debated by psychobiologists. They are asking if such things as television and video games have actually altered human brain structures, but no concrete results have yet been obtained.

8. Poet R. S. Thomas, in one of his most haunting recent works, cries out: "The machine is everywhere and is young. / How can I find God?" Untitled in *Counterpoint* (Newcastle-upon-Tyne, U.K.: Bloodaxe Books, 1990), p. 53.

9. *Urban Fortunes: The Political Economy of Place* (Berkeley: University of California Press, 1987), p. 62. See also "The Machine as an Icon of Economic Growth" in S. MacDonald, D. Lamberton, and T. Mandeville, eds., *The Trouble With Technology: Explorations in the Process of Technological Change* (New York: St Martin's, 1983), pp. 142-57. Peter Mathais argues that the machine continues to be such a powerful image that we have real difficulty conceptualizing economic growth in any other terms than as a growth in the number and efficiency of machines. This, Mathais claims, has actively inhibited growth in the service-sector.

10. See Frederich Klemm, *A History of Western Technology* (New York: Scribner, 1959), pp. 88-93. De Honnecourt proposed a wheel fitted with weights and lodestones that had a myriad of subsidiary uses, one of which was notably "liturgical": "In this fashion," says de Honnecourt, "one builds an angel whose finger points always toward the sun. . . . In this fashion one makes an eagle that always turns his head toward the deacon when he is reading the Gospel."

11. Jacob Leupold, *Theatricum Machinarum hydraulicum* (Leipzig, 1725). Cited in Klemm, p. 235. Emphasis added.

12. Cited in Lewis Mumford, *The Condition of Man* (New York: Harcourt, Brace and Co., 1944), p. 305.

13. Frank Lloyd Wright, "The Art and Craft of the Machine" in *Frank Lloyd Wright: Writings and Buildings* (New York: Horizon, 1969), p. 130.

14. Franz Reuleaux, *Theoretische Kinematik: Grundzüge zur Theorie des Machinewesens* (Brunswick, 1875), p. 234. Cited in Schivelbusch, *The Railway Journey*, pp. 169-70.

15. Samuel Butler, *The Note-books of Samuel Butler* (London, 1919).

16. Brian Wren (1936-), *Hymns and Psalms* (London: Methodist Publishing House, 1983), hymn number 351. The third stanza of this hymn (revised by the author since publication in the hymnal) runs: "Praise God for the harvest of alloy and ore, By mining and drilling on land and off-shore; For oil and for iron, for tinplate and coal, Praise God, who in love has provided them all." Copyright 1978 by Hope Publishing Company, Carol Stream, IL 60188. All rights reserved, used by permission.

17. Timothy L. Smith, *Revivalism and Social Reform* (Nashville: Abingdon, 1957), p. 226.

18. Edward Beecher, "The Nature, Importance, and Means of Eminent Holiness Throughout the Church," *The American National Preacher X* (1835), pp. 193-94. This kind of optimism persisted throughout the next century. On January 16, 1920, on the occasion of the introduction of Prohibition, the Reverend Billy Sunday preached a sermon in Norfolk, Virginia, declaring: "The reign of tears is over. The slums will soon be a memory. We will turn our prisons into factories and our jails into storehouses and corncribs. Men will walk upright now, women will smile and children will laugh. Hell will be forever rent." Cited in John Kobler, *Ardent Spirits*, p. 12.

19. See Bernard Weisberger, *They Gathered at the River* (Boston: Little, Brown, 1957). In England, Primitive Methodist revivalism traveled in a similar way down the Grand Union Canal from Manchester toward London.

20. Calvin Colton, *The History and Character of American Revivals* (London: F. Westley and A. H. Davis, 1832), pp. 170-72. Cited in David Waddel, *Law as Gospel* (Metuchen, N.J.: Scarecrow Press, 1985). Colton argued that revivals are successful when the leader "calculates the arithmetic of faith in God's engagements."

21. Ibid., p. 149. Finney (1792–1875), probably the greatest of the nineteenth-century revivalists, moved in 1834 from conducting revivals himself to lecturing about how to conduct revivals. His enormously popular revival textbook, *Lectures on the Revivals of Religion* (1835), details his own techniques for worship. The most recent work on Finney is Glen A. Hewitt, *Regeneration and Morality: A Study in Charles Finney, Charles Hodge, John Nevin, and Horace Bushnell* (Brooklyn: Carlton, 1991). For the place of revivalism in the mecahnical age see Robert Alan Wauzzinski, *God and Gold: Protestant Evangelicalism and the Industrial Revolution, 1820–1914* (Rutherford, Penn.: Fairleigh Dickinson University Press, 1993), p. 203.

22. James Oramel Peck, *How to Conduct a Revival* (New York: Eaton and Mains, 1884), p. 169. Peck goes on to say that "the preparation for a revival is but an intelligent adjustment of well-known and divinely-sanctioned agencies to the ends which are sought" p. 172.

23. Ibid., pp. 223-24.

24. Weisberger, *They Gathered at the River*, p. 176.

25. Finney, *Lectures on the Revivals of Religion*, p. 276.

26. The work of Walter Rauschenbusch (1861–1918) is particularly important in this regard. See especially *Christianizing the Social Order* (1912) and *A Theology for the Social Gospel* (1917). See also David R. Newman, *Worship as Praise and Empowerment* (New York: Pilgrim Press, 1988), pp. 77-78.

27. Cited in Christopher Lasch, *The True and Only Heaven: Progress and Its Critics* (New York: Norton, 1991), pp. 381-82.

28. The Roman Catholic counterpart to this was the close relationship between Catholic social teaching (embodied in the encyclicals *Rerum Novarum* [1891] and *Quardagesimo Anno* [1931]) and the early years of the liturgical movement. In this case, however, it was individuals and communities who needed to conform themselves to the deep meaning of the liturgy, rather than the liturgy needing to adjust to the needs of people. It was people transformed by the liturgy as it stood who would be.transforming society at large. More recently, the Church Growth movement, with its arsenal of techniques and strategies for increasing the numbers and level of commitment of congregations, has made worship an essential weapon in that arsenal.

29. Berger, et al., *The Homeless Mind* (New York: Vintage, 1973), pp. 32-33.

30. See above, p. 20.

31. Thomas P. Hughes, "Machines, Megamachines, and Systems," in Stephen Cutcliffe and Robert. C. Post, eds., *In Context: Essays in Honor of Melvin Kranzberg* (Bethlehem, Penn.: Lehigh University Press, 1989).

32. Lewis Mumford, *Technics and Civilization* (New York: Harcourt Brace, 1934), p. 145.

33. Ibid., p. 146.

34. James Hopewell, *Congregation: Stories and Structures* (London: SCM Press, 1988), pp. 23-24.

35. Certainly this seems to be the place of worship for those who are promoting the principles of the Church Growth Movement. See, for example, C. Peter Wagner, *Strategies for Church Growth* (Eastbourne, U.K.: Kingsway, 1988).

36. See, for example, David C. Olsen, *Integrative Family Therapy*, Creative Pastoral Care and Counseling Series (Minneapolis: Augsburg Fortress, 1993) and J. Haley, *Problem-Solving Therapy* (San Francisco: Jossey-Bass, 1976).

37. Eugene Rochberg-Halton, *Meaning and Modernity: Social Theory and the Pragmatic Attitude* (Chicago: Chicago University Press, 1986), p. 275.

38. For the relationship between the idea of the body as a machine and the growth and diversification of medical specialties, see Edwin Clarke and L. S. Jacyna, *Nineteenth-century Origins of Neuroscientific Concepts* (Berkeley: University of California Press, 1987).

39. Sigfried Giedion is particularly critical of specialization, not only in his own discipline, the history and philosophy of technology, but in the other arts and sciences as well. "The outstanding person of our period, and its stigma as well, is the specialist. He grows out of the split personality and the unevenly adjusted man."

("Vorlesungen Yale. Trowbridge Lectures 1941/1942." Cited in S. Cutcliffe and R. C. Post, *In Context*, p. 112).

40. The professionalization of ministry has been heavily criticized by Stanley Hauerwas and William Willimon in *Resident Aliens* (Nashville: Abingdon, 1989).

41. Jackson Carroll, *As One With Authority: Effective Leadership in Ministry* (Louisville, Westminster/John Knox, 1991), p. 51. Carroll points out that the exact *kind* of expertise expected of ordained ministers is denominationally determined, with Presbyterians valuing learned exposition of the faith, United Methodists interpersonal skills, Baptists expertise in methods of evangelism.

42. Thomas Sweetser, S. J., and Carol Wisniewski Holden, *Leadership in the Successful Parish* (New York: Harper & Row, 1987), p. 148. Compare the final words of this quotation with the Marx quotation above, note 33.

43. Ibid.

44. Robert Wuthnow, *The Restructuring of American Religion* (Princeton: Princeton University Press, 1988), p. 88.

45. Ibid., p. 89.

46. Edward Hicks, "4th month, 7th and 8th [1846]," *Memoirs of the Life and Religious Labors of Edward Hicks, Late of Newtown, Bucks County, Pennsylvania. Written by Himself* (Philadelphia: Merrihew and Thompson, 1851), pp. 147-148.

47. Roy Rappaport, "Ritual, Time, and Eternity," *Zygon* 27:1 (March, 1992), p. 25.

48. Ibid.

49. The most recent generation of services from the United Church of Christ is an example.

50. Leonel Mitchell, "The New Rubricism." Unpublished paper delivered to the 1990 meeting of the Anglican sub-group of the North American Academy of Liturgy.

51. Howard Galley's *The Ceremonies of the Eucharist* (Cambridge, Mass.: Cowley Publications, 1989).

52. Byron Stuhlman *The Prayer Book Rubrics Expanded* (New York: Church Hymnal Corporation, 1987).

53. Don Saliers and C. D. Hackett, *The Lord Be With You: A Handbook for Presiding in Christian Worship* (Cleveland, Ohio: OSL Publications, 1990).

54. Galley, *The Ceremonies of the Eucharist*, pp. 134-71. This highly regularized approach to liturgical participation extends to the laity, who are instructed to "a. Reverence the altar with a deep bow before taking their seats. . . . b. Kneel or stand for prayer. c. Stand at the entrance of the ministers" all the way to "x. Reverence the altar before leaving the church" pp. 39-40.

55. Ibid., p. xiv.

56. See R. William Franklin, "Guéranger: A View on the Centenary of His Death" in *Worship* 49 (1975), pp. 318-28.

57. See James F. White, *The Cambridge Movement* (Cambridge: Cambridge University Press, 1962).

58. This can be seen in the calls for a return to the cathedral as the spiritual and practical heart of each Anglican diocese in England and, in the Protestant

Episcopal Church in the United States, the building of cathedral churches (usually in neo-Gothic style) for the various dioceses as they were organized.

59. The first (French) edition of Baumstark's great work *Comparative Liturgy* appeared in 1940 (and Oxford, Mowbray, 1958). See especially Frederick Sommers West, "Anton Baumstark's Comparative Liturgy in Intellectual Context" (Unpublished Ph.D. dissertation, Notre Dame, 1988) and Paul Bradshaw, *The Search for the Origins of Christian Worship* (London: SPCK, 1990), pp. 57-62.

60. See Bradshaw, *The Search for the Origins of Christian Worship*, p. 57. "The basic flaw in [Baumstark's] approach was a failure to recognize a difference between nature and culture: whereas nature is generated genetically, culture is transmitted socially."

61. See, for example, E. Schillebeeckx, *Christ, the Sacrament of the Encounter with God* (London: Sheed and Ward, 1979).

7. TECHNOLOGICAL RISK AND TECHNOLOGICAL COMPLACENCY

1. Thomas Merton, from "Exploits of a Machine Age" in *Collected Poems* (London: Sheldon Press, 1978). Reprinted by permission of New Directions Publishing Corp., New York.

2. *Risk* is a relatively recent term, having come into the English language from Spanish where it was originally a nautical term meaning "to run into danger or go into a rock." It largely replaces the older concept of fate or fortune.

3. Anthony Giddens, *Modernity and Self-Identity: Self and Society in the Late-Modern Age* (Oxford: Polity Press, 1991), p. 122.

4. The marketing of nostalgia is a very interesting case. As Christopher Lasch points out, the nostalgic penchant for "indulging in handmade goods in a world dominated by machine production" (which exactly parallels the nostalgic interest in "the pastoral" which dominated the previous century) is a luxury only the favored can afford. It is technology that creates both the need for and the possibility of fulfillment of the nostalgic quest. Lasch argues that nostalgia "undermines our ability to make intelligent use of the past," *The True and Only Heaven: Progress and Its Critics* (New York: Norton, 1991), p. 82.

5. Peter Berger, *The Sacred Canopy* (Garden City, N.Y.: Doubleday, 1969), p. 24.

6. Robert Wuthnow, *The Restructuring of American Religion* (Princeton, N.J.: Princeton University Press, 1988), p. 286. A survey conducted yearly since 1973 has asked respondents to select the leading causes of problems in America. Fewer than one in ten said "too much technology," p. 277.

7. Henry Adams, *The Education of Henry Adams* (Boston, Houghton Mifflin, 1961). In the *Illustrated London News* (23 March, 1889), p. 356, the "Gallerie des Machines" in the 1889 Paris Exposition was described as a "sanctuary of Industry." See Bruce Sinclair "Technology on Its Toes: Late Victorian Ballets, Pagents, and Industrial Exhibitions" in Stephen Cutcliffe and Robert Post, eds. *In Context: History and the History of Technology: Essays in Honor of Melvin Kranzberg* (Bethlehem, Pa.: Lehigh University Press, 1989), pp. 71-82.

8. James Hopewell, "From Holy Meals to TV Dinners" in Barbara Brown Taylor, ed. *Ministry and Mission: Theological Reflections for the Life of the Church*, ed. Barbara Brown Taylor (Atlanta: Post Horn Press, 1985), p. 56.

9. Wuthnow, *The Restructuring of American Religion*, p. 286.

10. See ibid., pp. 206-7 and the chapter titled "Civil Religion to Technology" in ibid, pp. 268-96.

11. H. E. Fosdick, "On Worshipping Things we Manufacture" in *On Being Fit to Live With* (London: SCM Press, 1947), p. 120.

12. See Jonathan Schell, *The Fate of the Earth* (New York: Avon, 1982), pp. 118-29.

13. See, especially, David Ray Griffin, *Evil Revisited* (Albany, SUNY Press, 1991), especially chap. 1 "The Divine and the Demonic in a Holocaust," pp. 9-34. In *After Auschwitz: Radical Theology and Contemporary Judiasm,* (Indianapolis: Bobbs-Merrill, 1966), Richard Rubenstein argues that no one (but especially no Jew) can ever again believe in the biblical God of history. See esp. pp. 46, 48, 64-65.

14. In *The Evolution of Technology* (Cambridge: Cambridge University Press, 1988), George Basalla describes the repetitive cycle of "invention, replication, and discard" as the hallmark of the technological age. "Invention breaks the stale routine, replication makes the invention widely available, and discard assures that there will be room for newly invented things in the future," p. 187.

15. "Choruses from 'The Rock' " in *The Collected Poems 1909–1962*. Used by permission of Harcourt Brace Jovanavich and Faber & Faber, Ltd. D. H. Lawrence puts the problem of faith in a technological age in a slightly different way when he says that "Knowledge has killed the sun, making it a ball of gas with spots . . . The world of reason and science. . . . This is the dry and sterile world the abstracted mind now inhabits."

16. William Appleman Williams, cited in S. Cutcliffe and R. Post, *In Context*, p. 150. Media historian Joshua Meyrowitz describes the television as setting up "parasocial" communities. These mediated relationships with the people who inhabit the world of television resemble psychologically face-to-face interaction, and have their greatest impact on "the socially isolated, the socially inept, the aged, the timid and rejected." Meyrowitz, *No Sense of Place* (New York: Oxford, 1985), pp. 119-21.

17. Jacques Ellul, *The Technological Society* (New York: Knopf, 1964), p. 427.

18. See, for example, for Jewish theological responses to the Shoah, Marc Ellis, *Toward a Jewish Theology of Liberation* and Stephen Katz, *Post-Holocaust Dialogues* (New York: New York University Press, 1983); for efforts to reconstruct Christian theology after the Holocaust, see Griffin, *Evil Revisited* (Albany: SUNY Press, 1991); David Tracy, "Religious Values After the Holocaust" in *Jews and Christians After the Holocaust*, Abraham Peck, ed. (Philadelphia: Fortress, 1982) and James F. Moore, *Christian Theology After the Shoah* (New York: University Press of America, 1993).

19. Emil Fackenheim, "Holocaust" in *Contemporary Jewish Religious Thought*, ed. A. A. Cohen and P. Mendes-Flohr (New York: Free Press, 1987), p. 400. Compare this with the description of the characteristics of bureaucracy in chap. 3.

20. Elie Wiesel, *Night* (New York: Bantam, 1982), p. 136.

21. See Dow Marmur, *Beyond Survival: Reflections on the Future of Judaism* (London: Darton, Longman and Todd, 1982), especially chap. 18, "Work and Worship," pp. 130-40.

22. Ellis, *Toward a Jewish Theology of Liberation*, p. 27.

23. David Power, *Worship* 57:2 (1983), p. 328.

24. See Griffin, *Evil Revisited*, especially chapter 11, "Worship and Theodicy," pp. 196-213.

25. Moore, *Christian Theology After the Shoah*, p. 3.

26. On the mythic quality of television programming, see Gregor Goethals, *The Electronic Golden Calf: Images, Religion, and the Making of Meaning* (Cambridge, Mass.: Cowley Press, 1990), pp. 109-20.

27. Ibid., p. 120.

28. For a useful survey of religious television, see Peter G. Horsfield, *Religious Television: The American Experience* (New Brunswick, N.J.: Rutgers University Press, 1984).

29. For the rise of televangelism in this period, see Wuthnow, *The Restructuring of American Religion*, pp. 191-197.

30. Goethals, *The Electronic Golden Calf*, p. 175.

31. According to the Barna survey, of those who watched religious broadcasting, 53 percent were church attenders.

32. The practice of spiritual discipline has also followed this trend, with an increasing array of spiritual "techniques" available from which to choose, and a high degree of "brand switching" and "brand mixing" occurring.

33. Frank C. Senn, *Worship in Its Cultural Setting* (Philadelphia: Fortress Press, 1983), p. 57.

8. CHRISTIAN WORSHIP AND TECHNOLOGY IN DIALOGUE

1. John Calvin, *Institutes*, vol. I, trans. Henry Beveridge (Chicago: Encylcopedia Britannica, 1990), pp. 471-72 (3.2.4).

2. See Charles Davis, "Ghetto or Desert: Liturgy in a Cultural Dilemma" in *The Temptations of Religion* (London, 1973).

3. This is highlighted by the fact that so-called "technological societies" operate in quite different ways, and the place of Christian worship in one society will be quite different from that in another. For example, in the latest round of surveys, slightly less than half of the American population described themselves as "church-goers." At the same time, 4.7 percent of people surveyed in England would describe themselves in the same terms. The way in which technology interacts with liturgy is dependent upon a whole range of other cultural conditions and constraints. The relationship between highly technologized society and the extremely formal and stylized social and religious ritual in Japan has yet to be subjected to intensive study.

4. Hopewell, "From Holy Meals to TV Dinners," in Barbara Brown Taylor, ed., *Ministry and Mission: Theological Reflections for the Life of the Church* (Atlanta: Post Horn Press, 1985), p. 57.

5. Goethals, *The TV Ritual: Worship at the Video Altar* (Boston: Beacon Press, 1981), pp. 143-44.

6. Giddens, *Consequences of Modernity* (Stanford: Stanford University Press, 1992), p. 38.

7. Paul Ricoeur, "Civilization and National Cultures" in *History and Truth*, C. A. Kelbley, trans. (Evanston, Ill.: Northwestern University Press, 1965).

8. Lasch, *The True and Only Heaven: Progress and Its Critics* (New York: Norton, 1991), p. 48.

9. Ibid., p. 80.

10. Raymond B. Fosdick, "The Atomic Age and the Good Life" in *Within Our Power: Perspective for a Time of Peril* (New York: Longmans Green, 1952), p. 70.

SELECT BIBLIOGRAPHY

Aries, Philippe. *The Hour of our Death*. New York: Knopf, 1981.

Barbour, Ian. *Ethics in an Age of Technology*. London: SCM Press, 1992.

Barnard, Sylvia. *To Prove I'm Not Forgot: Death and Dying in a Victorian City*. Manchester: Manchester University Press, 1990.

Basalla, George. *The Evolution of Technology*. Cambridge: Cambridge University Press, 1988.

Bennett, Ivan Blackwell, Jr., *Methodism and Alcohol: Recommendations for a Beverage Alcohol Policy based on the Ever-changing Historic Disciplinal Positions of American Methodism*. Claremont, unpublished D.Min. thesis, 1973.

Berger, P., Berger, B., and Kellner, H. *The Homeless Mind*. New York: Vintage, 1973.

Blocker, Jack S. Jr. *American Temperance Movements: Cycles of Reform*. Boston: Twayne, 1989.

Borchert, D. M. and Stewart, D. (eds.) *Being Human in a Technological Age*. Athens: Ohio University Press, 1979.

Bosch, David. *Transforming Mission*. Maryknoll, N.Y.: Orbis, 1982.

Bouley, Allan. *From Freedom to Formula: The Evolution of the Eucharistic Prayer from Oral Improvisation to Written Texts*, CUA Studies in Christian Antiquity 21. Washington: Catholic University of America Press, 1981.

Bowman, LeRoy. *The American Funeral: a Study in Guilt, Extravagance, and Sublimity*. Washington: Public Affairs Press, 1959.

Bradshaw, Paul F. *The Search for the Origins of Christian Worship: Sources and Methods for the Study of Early Liturgy*. London: SPCK, 1992.

Brake, George Thompson. *Drink: Ups and Downs of Methodist Attitudes toward Temperance*. London: Oliphants, 1974.

Brooks, Chris. *Mortal Remains*. Exeter: Wheaton, 1989.

Brueggemann, Walter. *The Bible and the Postmodern Imagination*. Minneapolis: Augsburg Fortress, 1993.

Chadwick, Owen. *The Victorian Church.* London: Adam and Charles Black, 1966.

Chazanoff, William. *Welch's Grape Juice: From Cooperation to Cooperative.* Syracuse: Syracuse University Press, 1977.

Clebsch, William A. *From Sacred to Profane America: The Role of Religion in American History.* New York: Harper and Row, 1968.

Crockett, William R. *Eucharist: Symbol of Transformation.* New York: Pueblo, 1989.

Cross, Nigel; Elliott, David; and Roy, Robin, eds. *Man Made Futures.* London: Hutchinson, 1974.

Cutcliffe, Stephen and Post, Robert (eds.). *In Context: History and the History of Technology: Essays in Honor of Melvin Kranzberg.* Bethlehem, Pa.: Lehigh University Press, 1989.

Duffy, Eamon. *Stripping the Altars: Traditional Religion in England, c.1400 to c.1580.* New Haven: Yale University Press, 1992.

Eisenstein, Elizabeth. *The Printing Press as an Agent of Change.* Cambridge: Cambridge University Press, 1979.

Ellul, Jacques. *The Technological Society,* trans. J. Wilkinson. New York: Knopf, 1964.

———. *The Technological System,* trans. J. Neugroschel. New York: Continuum, 1980 (New York: Knopf, 1964).

Galley, Howard E. *The Ceremonies of the Eucharist: A Guide to Celebration.* Cambridge, Mass: Cowley Publications, 1989.

Giddens, Anthony. *The Consequences of Modernity.* Stanford: Stanford University Press, 1992.

———. *Modernity and Self-Identity: Self and Society in the Late Modern Age.* Cambridge: Polity Press, 1991.

———. *Sociology: A Brief but Critical Introduction* (2nd ed.). London: Macmillan, 1986.

Giedion, Sigfied. *Mechanization Takes Command.* New York: Oxford University Press, 1948.

Gimpel, Jean. *The Medieval Machine: The Industrial Revolution in the Middle Ages.* London: Book Club Associates, 1977.

Gittings, Clare. *Death, Burial, and the Individual in Early Modern England.* London: Croom Helm, 1984.

Goethals, Gregor. *The Electronic Golden Calf: Images, Religion, and the Making of Meaning.* Cambridge, Mass.: Cowley Publications, 1990.

———. *The TV Ritual: Worship at the Video Altar.* Boston: Beacon Press, 1981.

Griffin, David Ray. *Evil Revisited.* Albany: SUNY Press, 1991.

Hardman, Keith J. *Charles G. Finney, 1972–1875: Revivalist and Reformer.* Syracuse: Syracuse University Press, 1987.

Harvey, David. *The Condition of Post-Modernity.* Oxford: Blackwell, 1989.

Holeton, David R. *Liturgical Inculturation in the Anglican Communion* (Alcuin/GROW Liturgical Study 15). Bramcotte, Notts.: Grove Books, 1990.

Hopewell, James. *Congregation: Stories and Structures*. Minneapolis: Fortress Press, 1987.

Hopper, David H. *Technology, Theology, and the Idea of Progress*. Louisville: Westminster/John Knox, 1991.

Houlbrooke, Ralph (ed.). *Death, Ritual, and Bereavement*. London: Routledge, 1989.

Hughes, Thomas P. *American Genesis: A Century of Invention and Technological Enthusiasm, 1870–1970*. New York: Penguin, 1989.

Jacoby, Henry. *The Bureaucratization of the World* (tr. by Evelyn Kanes). Berkeley: University of California Press, 1973.

Jones, C.; Wainwright, G.; Yarnold, E.; and Bradshaw, P. (eds.). *The Study of Liturgy* (Rev. ed.). New York: Oxford University Press, 1992.

Jupp, Peter. *From Dust to Ashes: The Replacement of Burial by Cremation in England, 1840–1967*. London: Congregational Memorial Hall Trust, 1990.

Kavanagh, Aidan. *On Liturgical Theology*. New York: Pueblo, 1988.

Kobler, John. *Ardent Spirits: The Rise and Fall of Prohibition*. London: Michael Joseph, 1974.

Koprowski, Hilary, and Plotkin, Stanley A., *World's Debt to Pasteur: Proceedings of a Centennial Symposium Commemorating the First Rabies Vaccination* (Wistar Symposium Series, volume 3). New York: Alan R. Liss, 1985.

Kuhns, William. *The Post-Industrial Prophets: Interpretations of Technology*. New York: Harper & Row, 1971.

Landes, David. *Revolution in Time: Clocks and the Making of the Modern World*. Cambrdige: Harvard University Press, 1983.

Lasch, Christopher. *The True and Only Heaven: Progress and Its Critics*. New York: W. W. Norton, 1991.

Latour, Bruno. *The Pasteurization of France*. Cambridge: Cambridge University Press, 1988.

Lopez, Robert S. *The Commercial Revolution in the Middle Ages, 950–1350*. Cambridge and New York: Cambridge University Press, 1976.

Macey, Samuel L. *Clocks and the Cosmos: Time in Western Life and Thought*. Hamden, Conn.: Archon Books, 1980.

McLaughlin, William. *Revivals, Awakenings, and Reform: An Essay in Religious and Social Change in America, 1607–1977*. Chicago: University of Chicago Press, 1975.

Meyrowitz, Joshua. *No Sense of Place: The Impact of Electronic Media on Social Behavior*. New York: Oxford University Press, 1985.

Mitford, Jessica. *The American Way of Death*. New York: Simon and Schuster, 1963.

Moore, James F. *Christian Theology After the Shoah*. New York: University Press of America, 1993.

Morris, R. J. *Cholera, 1832: The Social Responses to an Epidemic*. London: Croom Helm, 1976.

Mumford, Lewis. *The Myth of the Machine*. New York: Harcourt Brace Jovanovich, 1966.

———. *Technics and Civilization*. New York: Harcourt Brace Jovanovich, 1934.

Newman, David R. *Worship as Praise and Empowerment*. New York: Pilgrim Press, 1988.

Ovitt, George. *The Restoration of Perfection: Labor and Technology in Medieval Culture*. New Brunswick, NJ: Rutgers, 1986.

Peck, Jonas Oramel. *Revival and the Pastor*. New York: Eaton and Mains, 1884.

Rappaport, Roy. "Ritual, Time and Eternity" in *Zygon* 27:1 (March, 1992), 5-29.

Richardson, Ruth. *Death, Dissection and the Destitute*. London: Penguin, 1988.

Rochberg-Halton, Eugene. *Meaning and Modernity*. Chicago: University of Chicago Press, 1986.

Rose, Margaret. *The Post-Modern and the Post-Industrial*. New York: Cambridge University Press, 1991.

Rosenwein, Barbara. "Feudal War and Monastic Peace: Cluniac Liturgy as Ritual Aggression" in *Viator* II (1971), pp. 129-57.

Senn, Frank C. *Christian Worship and Its Cultural Setting*. Philadelphia: Fortress, 1983.

———. *New Eucharistic Prayers: An Ecumenical Study of their Development and Structure*. New York: Paulist Press, 1987.

Skrade, Carl. *God and the Grotesque*. Philadelphia: Westminster Press, 1974.

Smith, Timothy L. *Revivalism and Social Reform in Mid-Nineteenth-Century America*. Nashville: Abingdon, 1957.

Spitz, Lewis W. "Model Man, Modern Man, Reformation Man" in *Continuity and Discontinuity in Church History* (Essays Presented in Honor of George Hunstan Williams). Leiden: Brill, 1979.

Stannard, D. E. *Death in America*. Philadelphia: University of Pennsylvania, 1976.

Stevenson, Kenneth (ed.). *Liturgy Reshaped*. London: SPCK, 1982.

Tames, Richard L. *Documents of the Industrial Revolution, 1750–1850*. London: Hutchinson Educational, 1971.

Taylor, Barbara Brown, ed. *Ministry and Mission: Theological Reflections for the Life of the Church*. Atlanta: Post Horn Press, 1985.

Taylor, Keith. *Henri Saint-Simon, 1760–1825*. London: Croom Helm, 1975.

Thompson, Kenneth A. *Bureaucracy and Church Reform: 1800–1965*. Oxford: Clarendon Press, 1970.

Thurian, Max (ed.). *Churches Respond to BEM*, volumes 1-6. Geneva: World Council of Churches, 1987.

Tillich, Paul. *The Spiritual Situation in our Technological Society*. Macon, GA: Mercer University Press, 1988.

Townsend, James W. "Communion Wine and Bible Temperance" (pamphlet). New York: American Temperance Society, 1872.

Trachtenberg, Alan. *Democratic Vistas 1860–1880*, chapter 13, "Perils of Mechanization." New York: Braziller, 1970.

Waddel, David. *The Law as Gospel: Revival and Reform in the Theology of Charles G. Finney*. London: Scarecrow Press, 1985.

Walker, George Alfred. *Gatherings from Grave-yards: particularly those of London; with a concise history of the modes of interment among different nations, from the earliest periods*. London, 1839.

Watt, Tessa. *Cheap Print and Popular Piety, 1550–1640* (Cambridge Studies in Early Modern British History). Cambridge: Cambridge University Press, 1991.

White, Lynn Jr. "Cultural Climates and Technological Advance in the Middle Ages" in *Viator* 2 (1975), 171-202.

————. *Medieval Religion and Technology: Collected Essays*. Berkeley: University of California Press, 1978.

————. *Medieval Technology and Social Change*. Oxford and New York: Oxford University Press, 1962.

————. "Medical Astrologers and late-Medieval Technology" in *Viator* 6 (1975), 295-308.

Worgul, George. *From Magic to Metaphor: A Validation of the Christian Sacraments*. New York: Paulist Press, 1980.

Wuthnow, Robert. *The Restructuring of American Religion: Society and Faith Since World War II*. Princeton: Princeton University Press, 1988.

INDEX

INDEX OF PERSONS

SUBJECT INDEX

INDEX